RECOVERY FOR MALE VICTIMS OF CHILD SEXUAL ABUSE

BY
HANK ESTRADA

To inquire about scheduling Hank Estrada for speaking engagements, you may write to him at the address below.

Hank Estrada
Red Rabbit Press
P.O. Box 6545
Santa Fe, New Mexico 87502-6545

Second Edition 1994
First Edition 1990

Design by H. Estrada and A.R. Garcez
Photos by A.R. Garcez

Library of Congress Catalog Card Number 90:61390

ISBN Number 0-9634029-1-9

Dedication

To those who suffer in silence:

Be not afraid of going slowly,
be afraid only of standing still.

Table of Contents

Foreword

For years male survivors of child sexual abuse could find few reliable resources addressing their abuse issues specifically. Mostly, information about sexual abuse had a female focus. Males were thought of as perpetrators, not victims of sexual abuse. Males were also very reluctant to disclose sexual victimization experiences. Thus, little was really known about the sexually maltreated male.

But something important is happening. Male survivors of child sexual abuse are breaking the silence about their victimizations. Now, increasing numbers of males are beginning to disclose their abuse experiences to parents, partners, friends, clergy, practitioners and to each other. While it may remain a challenge for many in our society to admit that child sexual abuse is not for females only, virtually no one can deny that sexual abuse poses a significant risk to any child's well-being.

Recovery for Male Victims of Child Sexual Abuse memorializes one man's experience with child sexual abuse. Hank Estrada's story reflects the struggle most sexually abused males experience in their attempts to understand what happened to them and how the abuse affected their lives. It also offers hope that recovery is, indeed, possible. While this volume is not, nor was intended to be, the definitive work on treating male survivors, Hank both asks and answers most of the questions males have about their own child sexual abuse experiences. Hank's presentation is straight-forward and powerful. His story can provide an important reference point for males who are just starting out on their path to recovery. It can also serve as a valuable resource for others who plan to assist or accompany male survivors on their difficult, but ultimately rewarding, journey.

Hopefully, those who read *Recovery for Male Victims of Child Sexual Abuse* will be helped in their own quest for recovery. It is also hoped that Hank's story and the stories of other male survivors will find their way into all our consciousness. If so, perhaps we can work together to finally stop the sexual victimization of all children, regardless of gender.

Larry A. Morris, Ph.D.
Clinical Psychologist
Co-author, *Males at Risk: The Other Side of Child Sexual Abuse*

Recovery For Male
Victims of Child Sexual Abuse

Hank, explain what happened to you as a child.

I was sexually abused by an uncle who happened to be the family's favorite baby-sitter. It began when I was four. My mother, it seems, was always busy trying to take care of household chores and us children at the same time. I was the eldest of five children, and my father was often a violent and abusive alcoholic during these years. When my uncle would volunteer to lay me down for daily afternoon naps, my mother was more than willing to accept his "generous offer."

During these nap times, while my uncle and I would lie together, he would begin stroking and caressing me while holding me close to his body. This became a daily occurrence. Gradually the caressing developed into sexual play. I was persuaded to touch and kiss his erect penis and masturbate him. He attempted anal intercourse, but due to the small physical size of my body, my uncle was not able to follow through. This sexual abuse continued for twelve years. By the time I reached sixteen I was severely depressed and confused over this "relationship." I seriously contemplated suicide.

Did your uncle say or do anything to both keep you quiet or gain your confidence?

My uncle would give me treats such as ice cream, candy and toys. He would take me to the park and push me on the swings. He would treat me to many of the things I enjoyed, such as pulling me on my wagon. He did things for me that my parents or older adults did not have the time to do. My uncle would also tell me how special I was to him and how he loved me. If I wanted anything at all, he would promise to get it for me. He reminded me over and over, I was his "special" nephew. Given this status, I felt in my own childlike thinking that I could not betray his affection without risking the loss of the many toys and treats, or his ever-ready attention.

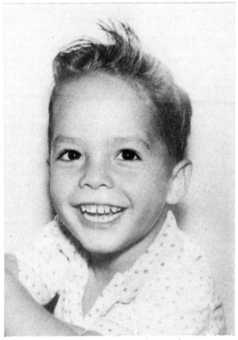

Sexual molestation began at age 4.

Were you able to tell anyone what was happening between you and your uncle?

No. . .I was afraid of getting my uncle and myself into trouble. I was also afraid that if my parents were to find out about us, they would not want me or that I would be abandoned. I was especially afraid of my father. He was an alcoholic, and periodically, he would get into violent, physical fights with my mother and later with me. I was afraid he would seriously harm my uncle if he learned of the abuse, for I truly loved my uncle. He had the exact opposite personality from my father. My uncle presented himself as patient, gentle, supportive, and affectionate—qualities which my father seldom revealed to me. And so, I ended up protecting my uncle, and thereby, protecting the only feeling of love that I could identify with. This, of course, was a distorted view.

As a child, did you send out clues or messages for your parents to pick up regarding the abuse?

No. Unfortunately in my family alcoholism played a large part in my not being able to openly communicate my feelings to my parents. My father was unapproachable because of his continuous alcohol abuse. My mother desperately tried to keep the family together even if it meant consciously ignoring such a traumatic issue as my abuse. I was aware of this unspoken rule even at a young age. My parents always were too preoccupied with paying bills and providing a home, school clothes, and food. This was made very clear as financial concerns were the source of many arguments between my parents. How could I go to them with my problems? They had too many of their own. Besides, I was led to believe by my father that I was a large part of the problem. So much pressure, stress, and tension existed in the family, that my reaction was to simply keep quiet. I felt I could only "wish" my abuse and other family problems away. This was how I coped.

A happy young boy?

Hank, victims of child abuse sometimes say they remember little of their childhood. Have you experienced a similar loss of memory?

I remember moments of my childhood, but, aside from the sexual abuse, I don't remember much. Most of my recollections tend to be of a childhood that was traumatic, of a family life enclosed in secrecy, alcohol abuse, and violence. To this day I experience gaps in my memory that are constant reminders of the emotional pain and distress that, as a child, I had to endure. For the longest time, I thought that my abuse began when I was seven. Recently, I was casually browsing through a family photo album and discovered a photograph of the house where most of the abuse took place. I looked at the date written on the photograph and suddenly realized I was four years old when the abuse began three years

4

younger than I had previously thought. Somehow, I had blocked the memory of a three year span of my childhood. I was faced with the difficult process of somehow recovering those three lost years.

So, I have experienced the type of memory repression that is a common symptom of child abuse, firsthand. Frequently, in adult life, a flashback relating to the abuse will suddenly occur when triggered by something that is unconsciously associated with the childhood trauma. Recently, I walked past the linens section in a local department store. For some reason my attention was drawn to a display of a child's bedroom ensemble. Everything in the room matched—the bedspreads, pillow cases, drapes, even the carpets were decorated in an earthtone plaid. Suddenly, I felt nauseous and my limbs weakened. At that instant, I recalled the nightmare of my own sexual abuse as I realized that it took place in a bedroom decorated with the same identical designs. I had completely repressed the memory associated with my bedroom and abuse.

Aside from sexual abuse, what other forms of child abuse exist?

There are several forms—verbal, emotional and physical abuse. **Verbal abuse** takes place when a parent screams threats, insults, and obscenities at a child. Whenever my father drank, he always had something abusive to say. He frequently told me, "You disgust me, and if you ever get in my way, I'll kill you." I believed him.

Emotional abuse can be used in subtle but vicious ways. When he was sober, my father gave me money and complimented me for being helpful around the house. But within an hour, after a few shots of whiskey, he would summon me and lecture me about my "laziness" and "smart-assed attitude." I often felt like a ping-pong ball being whacked back and forth across a table, never knowing what to believe, uncertain of how he actually felt about me.

The most visibly recognizable form is **physical abuse.** A child with scars, bruises, cuts, burns, even dislocated or broken bones should always be regarded with the suspicion that they might be abused. Less physically identifiable but more frequent forms of physical abuse involve slapping, shoving, or shaking a child violently. Hair or ear pulling is common. In our home, my father resorted to various methods of "discipline." He would shake us violently at times. Sometimes he would forcibly grab and pull me by the arm. When I was twelve, I vividly recall defending my mother from my father during one of his drunken assaults. He slapped my face up against a sliding glass door. "I dare you to start crying," he muttered with clenched teeth as the tears welled in my eyes. They never fell.

Can anyone truely be trusted?

Is there a difference between being abused by a family member or acquaintance verses a stranger?

Yes, there is a difference. A pre-existing relationship of intimacy and trust exists with a family member, be it a mother, father, sister, brother, or, as in my case, an uncle. With a stranger the intense emotions of intimacy and trust do not exist. Yet, a child can develop a friendship with an authority figure such as a teacher, doctor, or clergyman which does not pre-exist as with a family member. When a family member violates a child, connected by blood or marriage, the level of abuse is intensified with the condition of their relationship. However, this level of intense closeness does not exist with a stranger. The abuse might be equal in manner, but not equal psychologically. Emotional confusion plays a large degree in abuse when perpetrated by a family member. Understandably, the long term effects are enormous on a child who has been taught and directed to love and trust an individual who later sexually abuses that child.

What happens if the perpetrator of sexual abuse is a woman?

Its a double situation for a boy. As a boy matures and learns his societys definition of what a "man" is, the reality of his abuse becomes even more confusing. Men in our society are expected to explore and be ready for sex all the time, provided it is "normal" sex with a female. First, the abuse by a woman on a male child is romanticized and defined as an initiation into manhood. On the other hand, if the child enjoys any part of it, he might not perceive the incident as abusive. If the experience was not enjoyable, the boy might develop a confusing sexual self image and most often think of himself as being gay.

The consequences of being abused either by a woman or a man remains the same later in life. It may be manifested as a sexual dysfunction, a lack of trust, or a negative self-image. If the perpetrator is the boys mother, it is more likely that the memories will be blocked mentally by the child. Because a mother is supposed to be all protecting and nurturing, the child may rationalize the abuse to the point it is forgotten or that it "never happened."

Is being abused once enough to qualify a person as being a victim?

Once is enough to leave an impression on a child. One act of abuse can traumatize a person physically and emotionally. Society must view every alleged act of abuse as serious. By the same token, a child's testimony of having been abused should not be trivialized.

Is it typical for the victim to keep quiet and simply carry this knowledge throughout life?

Yes, it is very typical. Among the most common reasons are guilt, shame, and fear. The conscious act of keeping quiet is often an attempt by the victim to cope with the abuse. In my situation, as a child, my right to tell was taken away by an adult whom I trusted and loved. I feared telling friends and classmates because they would know how "evil and sick" I was for having sex with my uncle. I feared telling my parish priest and religious instructors because if they knew, God would stop loving me and I would never be accepted in church or heaven.

School, a safe temporary distraction from home.

I feared telling my teachers because they would certainly want to discuss the matter with the police. I would then have been in serious trouble with my father. He would have beaten me to death since it involved his own brother. This made it difficult to love and trust people who said they loved and trusted me. None of them could help or save me. I was alone.

My response, and the typical response of others in my situation remained the same; I kept the violation to myself. I hoped that by not disclosing the abuse, it would simply go away. One can understand then the mixed emotions that confront an abused child. These emotions, however, do not disappear. They build and eventually become irrepressible.

Does society accept the image of males as victims of sexual abuse?

No, not completely. The reality of men as victims in our culture is still not totally accepted. For most people, the term "victim" conjures up images of a "helpless female" being confronted by a male assailant. To have been victimized as a child, an adult male must confront various prevalent "mind sets." Our culture also influences males to think of sex in terms of whether it was easy to get, rather than if it was a negative experience. Boys are often told, "Why complain? You just started earlier than most boys. Aren't you the lucky one?"

Age: 5 years.

We must combat social attitudes regarding male victimization and realize that boys are innocent victims and rarely are willing participants. Re-education is part of the recovery process that we, as abused males, must confront every time we elect to speak openly about our abuse. When a boy is victimized he is treated and often perceives himself as less than a man, effeminate, weak, or inferior. Men are expected to deal directly, confront and control any adverse situation, even if they are boys. Society, then, must develop a more objective view of the abuse of males if prevention and recovery are to be attained. The importance of open dialogue, clinical research, and accessibility to qualified professional therapists directly will assure the validity of the male as a victim of childhood abuse.

Is it possible that an element of society might view the sexual abuse of a boy as enjoyable to the child?

Yes, but please let me clarify this matter. While we must acknowledge that the victim can have a degree of pleasurable feelings during the time of abuse, the aftermath is traumatic. During the time I was being abused, I felt it was wrong; that it was my fault. But, because I was a developing adolescent, there were times that I experienced physical arousal and pleasure. This conflict of feelings led to a very negative self image. I grew more and more confused about what appropriate sexual behavior was.

Unfortunately, a portion of society perceives the sexual abuse of young males as positive. Although not a large portion, it is a number that must be addressed. This is crucial in the case of individuals who have influence or hold public office, like physicians, attorneys, judges, law enforcement and government officials. The decisions of an uninformed person of influence could obviously be prejudicial and harmful to child abuse cases particularly those in a court of law.

Therefore, to consider that a child would enjoy abuse is a way of denying that abuse exists. A child should not have to pay a price for love, touching, caressing, and hugging by having it sexualized.

As a teenager, how did you cope?

It was difficult facing the circumstances that surrounded my life. I was faced with a violent alcoholic father, a sexually abusive uncle and the responsibility of protecting my four younger brothers and sisters. I went through a great deal of emotional turmoil regarding my family. At school, I was a model student, the perfect example of a high achiever to instructors and my classmates. Never did I give a hint of my dysfunctional family life. At home, I never questioned authority. When told to do something, I did it without hesitation.

Age 12, father's alcoholism escalates to violent episodes of physical abuse.

This was also the case with my family. Whenever we were in public or at family gatherings, we all pretended as if everything was fine. We laughed, we talked, we played, we danced at relatives' homes. We were raised to be polite, respectful, and helpful children. This Jekyll and Hyde lifestyle became unbearable for me. At sixteen, with no end in sight to my despair and misery I seriously contemplated suicide. The attempt was unsuccessful. I then sought help at a local free clinic that offered counseling services. Looking for other support I eventually became involved in my high school Christian prayer group. These two resources helped me cope with the turmoil at home.

Does being sexually abused by a male affect the sexual preference of a boy later as an adult?

There is no clinical research to support the idea that once abused by a man the individual will become bisexual or gay. Straight-heterosexual men who were abused as children worry if they are gay. Gay men wonder if being abused as a child made them gay. Also, gay men have expressed anxiety wondering if they were abused because they were originally gay.

Many men engage in promiscuous, compulsive behavior with both men and women due to unresolved psychological and emotional needs. But, I want to stress that, in my opinion, being sexually abused by a male perpetrator does not automatically mean that a boy will grow up to be gay. Individuals must clarify many factors regarding sexual preference for themselves to be totally comfortable. To make a value judgement as to whether one lifestyle is better than another, or one is good or bad, is not a healthy approach. A man must carefully consider what he is comfortable with, what lifestyle he wants to pursue, and what type of life he wants for himself. He must be cautious about conforming to a standard established by society as being "normal." The objective opinions of a qualified therapist can be instrumental in assisting an individual in the clarification of his sexual preference and identity.

Age 16, tormented and desperate to the point of contemplating suicide.

What are some of the things that a male survivor of sexual abuse carries with him into adulthood?

One of the key consequences of being abused as a child is a serious lack of trust towards adults and authority figures. This happens particularly when the perpetrator is a close family member, someone the child loved, someone the child looked up to, someone who expressed love verbally while being sexually involved at the same time with the child. An internal conflict develops as to what "love" means and how it is expressed. Trusting someone later as an adult becomes confusing to the victim of sexual abuse. Understanding the concept of love can be difficult to comprehend. A sexually abused adult male finds it difficult to make new friends and keep them. Problems with intimacy occur, a result of repressed, negative associations which are unconsciously triggered by the possibility of an intimate encounter.

Male victims of abuse may create mental walls between themselves and their past; they become numb to their feelings. Adult survivors resort to a number of numbing strategies which involve alcohol, drugs, compulsive sex, and eating disorders. Others choose more socially acceptable forms of coping. Some become workaholics, super body-builders, and ultra marathon runners. They try to both numb and compensate for the pain, which in turn protects them from the memories of abuse.

As a result of keeping our abuse a secret, male survivors often develop negative self images. Some of us consider ourselves stupid, ugly, weak, disturbed and sick. Children and adults have carried the mental anguish that, they would not have been abused in the first place if they were more intelligent or better looking.

The effect that I personally carried into adult life was not being able to trust both men and women. Trust was something violated in my childhood. To love and be loved, to be involved in an intimate relationship emotionally and physically was difficult because of my experience of sexual abuse as a child. Therapy proved helpful in tearing down the walls that I had built to protect myself emotionally.

It is important to understand that there is hope for a male victim of sexual child abuse. But you must seek assistance by either meeting with other male survivors to share your experiences or participating in therapy with a qualified professional. You must know that you are not alone. "Healing yourself is possible."

Some people have said that survivors exhibit either a very serious personality or a "life of the party" personality. What are your observations?

I think most of us survivors have both a serious and funny side to our personality. Some of us use the silly and playful approach to distract us from looking directly at something that maybe affecting us emotionally. We thrive on the attention we were able to generate when being humorous and seemingly carefree. It seems as though when we experience a positive response from others, we feel liked and "normal". When others appear to be enjoying our antics, we feel like we "fit-in". The only problem that may arise with this type of behavior is that painful issues in ones personal life may not be getting the attention and resolve necessary for healing. I am concerned with an individual who constantly has to be telling jokes or performing "tricks", or laughing for any reason even when it's not appropriate.

On the other hand, being extremely serious and not ever showing a smile or laughing can be uncomfortable as well. As a child I learned to take everything very seriously and with great caution. Consequently, I've been told by friends and family to "lighten-up" and "chill-out" due to my being easily distressed and overcome by anxiety.

I learned very young that I needed to organize everything around me, including my own behavior, and to always be prepared for the worst. I never knew what I could do to prevent my father from becoming angry and violent with me. It seemed impossible for me to prevent his attacks, no matter how much I controlled my surroundings or behavior. Because of the constant threat of danger and violence in my life, I was unable to know how to relax or have fun and play as other neighborhood children did. Consequently, as an adult I am often uncomfortable around people having fun, telling jokes or acting silly. I have been able to overcome some of this with patient encouragement and support from people who understand. When we are able to surround ourselves with supportive and trusted friends, its a little easier to attempt to "let our guards down" and experience something pleasurable or fun. Unfortunately, we survivors of childhood traumas will always have to push ourselves just a bit more than others in order to overcome the occasional awkwardness of day to day living. It is possible, but you have to want to help yourself.

Did being an abused child affect your relationships later as an adult?

Yes, particularly during my college years. As a child I erroneously learned that in order to be loved, I had to perform something sexual. This reasoning stayed with me. As a result of this early training, later as an adult, I found myself acting in an unusual manner.

My college years, as for many students, were a time to explore and develop sexually. On several occasions, I became involved sexually with fellow classmates and instructors. I reasoned at the time, that in order to maintain any sense of friendship or to retain their interest in me as a person, I had to initiate something sexual between us. I believed my sexual ability would provide the only reason anyone would be interested in me. And so, establishing long-term friendships was impossible.

The few that did develop during these years were subsequently ended, due to this childhood understanding of what it meant to be physical with, liked and accepted by, another person. I believed that if people did not want sex from me, it was because I was not good enough. For me, love had to include sex, a way of thinking that I carried with me into adulthood.

It has taken years of self examination and discovery to realize that love need not be qualified with a sexual act, and that sex should not be confused with love. At present, I attribute my continuing recovery to the fact that I can talk openly about my insecurities and concerns with my partner, share mutual experiences with fellow survivors, and know that, ultimately, recovery is possible.

Given understanding and support, healing is possible.

Is it thought that men who were abused as children do themselves become abusers?

Unfortunately, this is a gross generalization and a common fallacy. Not all men who were abused as children become abusers. On the contrary, many tend to become protectors of children. They become teachers and social workers; they choose "protective" careers. These men make the solemn vow as children, "I am going to make damn sure that what happened to me, will not happen to another child." This is exactly what has sparked me in my effort to educate society regarding male victims of child sexual abuse.

The belief that sexually abused males become abusers is based on a few statistical studies conducted in prisons or correctional environments that house sexual offenders. These limited studies have spawned this erroneous impression that all survivors are degenerate walking "time bombs" set to go off at the first opportunity to abuse a child.

This prevalent attitude has hampered efforts to unite male sexual abuse survivors. As a group, we the "non-offending" male survivors must not be overlooked. We are a population that is much larger than most realize. Many are involved in "protective" situations. I base this on my personal observation and from the numerous phone calls and letters I have received from across the U.S. and Canada. But we have been held back by the fear that society will automatically assume that we, too, will abuse children.

There is a definite need for more in-depth study and research into the area of "non-offending" male survivors of childhood sexual abuse. At present there is an overwhelming lack of information. It is no wonder that men are uncomfortable exploring positive avenues of recovery when they find themselves frustrated and fearful over any attempt at disclosure.

Why use the term "survivor"?

We use the term to signify that recovery from childhood abuse is possible. Through all the hurt and abuse that we experienced as male children and adults, we continued to survive and overcome the isolation, shame, and fear. As adults, we have the responsibility to aid and support fellow survivors. We must help them reach a comfortable level of self-acceptance, confidence, and positive mental health. Personally, the term gives me a sense of accomplishment and a feeling of hope. I am aware that surviving childhood abuse is an ongoing process which will challenge me throughout my adult life. I know the risks of disclosing my personal history, but the rewards and inner peace I've achieved thus far are immeasurable. Yes, I am a survivor and I invite others to join me in recovery.

Should survivors confront their perpetrators?

This is a choice the individual must make after very careful consideration. A substantial amount of mental and emotional preparation must take place before a survivor attempts to confront his perpetrator. The foremost reason is to prevent further victimization that may be continued by the perpetrator in a number of ways. Perpetrators may rely on the emotional and psychological mastery that they previously held over the victim. They may deny any connection with the survivor's attempts at disclosing the abuse to avoid confrontation. They may even gain the trust and favor of family and friends and turn these people against the survivor.

It is therefore essential that adequate psychological preparation and emotional support exist. The survivor's fears, concerns, and actions should be discussed with a qualified therapist. It is imperative that the individual talk with other survivors who have confronted their perpetrators. I advise role-playing the various scenarios that may transpire during the confrontation. Survivors must remind themselves about what they expect the confrontation will accomplish and what reactions or responses they will have if they do not receive the answers they anticipate.

The confrontation with my uncle occurred unexpectedly one afternoon while we were both visiting my parents. He was accustomed to leaving the house whenever I arrived. I never acknowledged his presence, yet, he would always greet me with a guilty and cautious "Hello." He went out of his way to be the "nice guy" in front of everyone, while I was regarded as a cold, rude, and inconsiderate nephew. No one knew of our sexual relationship; they only observed our external behavior. I resented being thought of as the "bad guy." All the while my uncle glowed in the eyes of relatives and friends, an angel of innocence.

On this particular afternoon I exploded in disgust at his "holier than thou" behavior. I cornered him in the garage when we were alone. I was shaking with rage. My stomach convulsed as I stared directly into his eyes.

I pointed my finger in his face as I slowly threatened, "If I ever hear about you touching anyone, I will. . ." I never finished the sentence.

After what seemed an eternity of staring and silence I continued, "Do you understand what I am saying?"

In shock he nodded, "yes. . ?"

I squeezed my hand into a fist, held it close to his face, then turned and walked away.

My confrontation with my uncle was spontaneous. Those who decide to confront their perpetrator should prepare a final statement to close and terminate the confrontation. Ideally, this statement should be a clarification to announce the following:

1. The perpetrator is responsible for everything that took place.

2. The victim did not deserve the abuse.

3. The victim must acknowledge that in no way was he responsible for what happened.

Finally, it should be stressed, many survivors have recovered without ever confronting their perpetrators. They have found their own method of coping and source of refuge. Confronting the perpetrator is not necessarily for everyone, but for some, it has proven instrumental in their recovery.

What are some of the ways that men who were abused as boys can get help and support?

Men need to be aware that recovery from childhood abuse is possible. An individual begins the process by initially breaking his silence and talking about his child abuse experience. It is important to engage in therapy on a regular basis to deal specifically with the traumas created by the abuse. The next step is to share his experience with other survivors through self help, therapy and support groups. In addition, I strongly recommend that survivors read books and other literature about recovery from childhood abuse. Many outline the recovery process to help survivors understand it. If you currently have a drug or alcohol dependency, or compulsive behavior problems like eating, masturbation, or promiscuity, these addictions need to be controlled before the sexual abuse recovery process begins. These addictions/behaviors are serious obstacles to recovery. They tend to limit physical and emotional capacities for change. Lastly, there is no one single approach or guidelines to follow. The needs and capabilities of the individual will dictate the order which he will find most comfortable. I would tell a survivor: ultimately, you are the one in control of your recovery process. You decide at what pace to proceed. If you have not told anyone about your abuse, find someone you trust. If you have told someone, continue to seek support with your recovery.

Hank, what caused you to break your silence?

After 25 years of silence about being abused by my uncle, after convincing myself that I was his only victim, he attempted to sexually molest one of my nephews. By remaining silent all those years, I had inadvertently protected my uncle and allowed him the opportunity to claim another child victim. I felt a tremendous amount of guilt, pain, and rage. **I had to speak out to stop any further abuse.**

My first concern was to convince my nephew of his innocence in the incident. I offered him support by relating my sexual abuse experience, one we both shared with the same uncle. After talking with my nephew, I approached the other members of my immediate family individually. Denial, shock, doubt, anger and helplessness best describe their reactions.

This personal disclosure has not been without difficulty or controversy. I have since become an outcast from my entire family. I have become the villain in their eyes for betraying a family secret in an attempt to protect others and prevent further molestations. I am now treated as though I were the perpetrator and offender. To this day, no action has been taken by my immediate family members to get assistance, rehabilitation, or therapy for the perpetrator, the victims (and there have been more discovered), or others associated with the

Step forward, speak out and declare your freedom!

molestation. As far as I know, my uncle still has access to children and continues to be protected by relatives. Even more ironically, he is protected by laws which require that perpetrators be caught "in the act of committing" sexual molestation versus his past history of abuse and the testimony of other victims.

What ultimately made you decide to speak out about your childhood victimization?

I was often frustrated by my family's denial and silence over the traumatic environment in which we lived. After

I first told about my sexual history with my uncle, I was made to feel like the offender for identifying my abuser, and I also felt like a victim for admitting I participated in sexual behavior with him. I felt helpless because I could not trust those family members who should have been my protectors, because they made it very clear that talking about it was unacceptable. No one wanted to discuss the issue. Once the authorities had completed their investigation, the situation was never discussed again. I felt forced once again to remain silent about my traumatic experiences. For the longest time I felt completely isolated. I was blamed for speaking out.

It took me years of frustration to learn that most of those family members who remained silent, including my own father, had themselves been victims of some form of child abuse. These relatives were too wounded and scared to help me beacuse they never confronted their own painful childhood traumas. My anger and frustration turned to sorrow for them because they were never given the opportunity to seek help. They spent most of their adult lives in pain and sorrow. My anger returned once again when I took it upon myself to search out recovery resources nearest these family members, and they chose not to pursue the leads. At this point I realized that I could not help people who did not think they needed help, nor could I convince them that they had been child victims and now needed change in their adult lifestyles. I quickly realized that I needed to focus my energy on myself. I needed to help myself first before I could attempt to help anyone else. I made the decision to "let go" of my family and their mental health issues, and I stopped getting caught up in their complaining about all the "family problems" they had. My feeling was that they were now adults who did not want help.

They could not even admit there were serious problems that needed change, so I chose to separate myself from them. I then became determined to do everything I could, including speaking out publicly, to prevent further family sexual secrets from devouring other children.

So much energy is spent to sort out those family problems which inevitably resurface time and time again. It's the vicious cycle we often find ourselves attacking when unresolved family issues are denied and ignored. It is easy to get caught up in these cycles and to let ourselves feel guilty for not helping those in need. The problem with this is that these family members will always be "in need" and more than likely, will continue rehashing the same problems over and over again. The best advise I can give is: put yourself first. Family relations come and go, some for the better, some for the worse, but ultimately you're left with *you* no matter what, so *you*, not your family, should be your number one priority. Many families are dysfunctional and this can be one of the biggest detriments to our emotional healing and recovery.

After years of therapy, why do so many male survivors still feel emotionally insecure or fragile when certain words or events are mentioned?

What happened to us as children will never be forgotten. From time to time, for one reason or another, our emotional scars get "scratched" and this is always painful. These mental and emotional memories evoke particular physical and psychological responses from past abusive experiences. I like to refer to these instances as getting my "buttons" pushed. These buttons can be triggered by something as simple as hearing a word or being at a certain place. I can recall two very dramatic experiences when negative memories surfaces after being triggered by a location or comment.

The first experience happened one afternoon when I was walking through a department store. I walked through a section of the store where a child's bedroom furniture was displayed. I glanced at a pine wood bunkbed set which had earthtone plaid bedspreads, matching curtains and pillows neatly adorned. As I passed the center of this display, I suddenly felt nauseous, light headed and began smelling a fowl but familiar odor. My stomach tightened in pain and my legs felt weak. I quickly sat down so as not to fall over anything. After a few moments, I realized I was experiencing sensations which I had when I was a child in a bedroom similar to the display at the department store. I had pine bunkbeds with orange, brown and yellow plaid bedspreads and matching curtains. These physical reactions and sensations were memories I had subconsciously buried of the sexual molestations which took place in my bedroom. The odor I was smelling was that of my uncle's penis and alcohol breath. My stomach was feeling exactly as it did when my uncle performed oral sex and attempted anal penetration on me. Terror, stomach cramps and near vomiting was what I experienced during these sexual encounters with my uncle. These same responses were also what I felt standing before the child's bedroom display in the department store. I was completely shocked by this experience and could not have anticipated the dramatic reactions to events buried deep within my mind. For days afterwards, I remained profoundly disturbed by these memories but found consolation and understanding with my therapist.

A second experienced occured when my partner said "I love you" in the middle of our love making. I became completely numb, lost my erection and had to physically get away. My partner was never more sincere or "in love" at that moment and was genuinely expressing love. For me, I was reminded about all those times my uncle told me "I love you" while performing oral sex, fondeling or masturbating me. I felt cheap and lied to by my uncle each time he said "I love you". When my partner said this to me during sexual intimacy, I froze and became that "dirty little boy", who did "nasty" things with his uncle. Again, my therapist assisted me and encouraged my partner and me to discuss this in depth so that neither of us would have to experience that negative reaction again during sexual intimacy.

As you can imagine, these reactions are confusing, frustrating and can cause tremendous tension between two people. It is important for survivors to recognize what their emotional "buttons" are and what sets them off. We need to try to be conscious of those situations which make us feel depressed, upset or angry. We need to explore these reactions and trace, if possible, those responses linked to past abuse experiences. Once these "buttons" are identified, we can practice moving beyond the emotional barricades, resulting from triggered memories. In order to move beyond these barricades we need to allow ourselves the right to "claim" these feelings by reprocessing our thoughts in the here and now. We then can begin a rational healthy response to our adult environment.

I have had to learn appropriate ways of expressing feelings of fear, anger, distress and disappointment. This remains an on-going exercise for me and requires daily practice. Most of us who have survived childhood sexual traumas are well aware of those places, situations and things which make us feel uncomfortable. For those

Age 37, confident and thriving.

of us who have been fortunate enough to experience healthy / constructive therapy, we can identify those things which connect us to our childhood pain and address them directly. The fact that I have spent over seven years in therapy does not exclude me from moments of emotional sorrow, pain or insecurity.

How do you cope with the stress and anxiety of birthdays and family holiday celebrations?

I make it a point to avoid any family gathering that causes me to feel anxious or uncomfortable. I have learned the hard way that it serves absolutely no purpose for me to suffer in silence at the awkwardness of dealing with dysfunctional family members. I usually find that after I leave a family gathering I'm far from relaxed or happy. Instead, I often feel irritable and upset. A person is often left feeling compromised and emotionally used after hours of maintaining an artificial grin and occasional superficial conversation. You must realize that you are not in a healthy or supportive environment. A majority of our relatives have decided to stay in their own protective world of denial. Being around these relatives makes you feel stuck in pain, anger and distrust. It becomes easier with time to learn to trust complete strangers, to learn to develop a mutual respect for one another and to offer unconditional support. These new found friends often become the source of "family" you had to give up.

You can now choose the "family" environment you want to be with during special celebrations. You chose only those gatherings which you feel are healthy and emotionally non-threatening. Life is too short to have to endure the painful memories experienced at family gatherings. It's better, whenever possible, to spend as much time as you can around postive, supportive and healthy people, especially during holiday celebrations. The Christmas and New Year holidays were often periods of great stress and trauma for me as a child, due to the emotional and physical violence I experienced. Today, with my partner, dear friends and associates, these celebrations are a completely new and wonderful experience.

My advice, though easier said than done, is to stop putting your family's happiness first. Instead start surrounding yourself with healthier and happier people. Your happiness and health must take precedence. You

deserve it. We survivors need to take better care of ourselves, or at least practice better ways of caring for ourselves. One of the more difficult task in focusing on our
happiness is overcoming the feelings of guilt and responsibility towards our family. There came a point for me
when I had done all that I could to help each member
in my family, but without success. I had to let go, to get
on with my life. The weight is lifted and I no longer feel
that my presence at gatherings is necessary to ensure
other people's happiness or good time. I also gained a
tremendous sense of self respect and esteem for my decision not to participate in affairs that were emotionally
unhealthy. I have control of how I spend my time now
and there is no more room for compromise or self-
sacrifice. I now control how, and with whom, I spend
my time. It's been extremely liberating.

If approached by a survivor for help, what issues should a non-victim consider?

For most people, especially non-victims, the subject of
child abuse causes some level of discomfort. As survivors, we are very much aware of this; we know these
feelings are unavoidable. But non-victims must be conscious of the element of privilege survivors give in choosing a confidant to share their story with. This individual
has been given the status of trust that has not been
granted to anyone else. The listener must be aware of
this. It is best for the listener not to give advice or be
judgmental or critical. The exchange tends to be more
productive if the non-victim simply listens and offers
support.

Listeners should also share what they feel in a genuine,
honest and sincere manner. For example, if at a loss for

words the listener should say so rather than remain silent. Silence in this situation may be interpreted as rejection. Under no circumstances should the survivor be advised to "forgive and forget" the abuse. Such well intentioned advice can be emotionally damaging and wrong. Be aware that most of us cannot "forgive" and it is impossible for us to "forget" the long term effects of our childhood abuse. Another response that often causes further harm is for individuals to say, "Leave it up to God, pray and it will go away." This "re-victimizes" the survivor by implying that he would have been saved the abuse if he had called upon God in the first place.

Many victims of abuse, as children, spent countless hours praying to be "rescued" and were disappointed. I am not saying that prayer is not valid in recovery; it has helped many. Placing a sectarian value judgement, however, on the shoulders of a victim / survivor is not a healthy approach.

Hank, what should parents know about child abuse and how can they prevent it?

Parents must listen to their children and communicate through honest discussions. Look for signs of unusual behavior, such as a new fear of people or places that were not previously feared. Parents should be aware of changes in school attendance, study, play or eating habits. In general, any sudden, suspicious changes, or mood swings, including depression, violence, and aggression, or the need to avoid social gatherings, may be indicators of a problem.

Parents must continually provide an atmosphere of trust and love. They must demonstrate a willingness to discuss any subject that their child initiates. Children should also feel free to talk with their parents without fear of judgement, reprimand or ridicule. Parents should also educate their children about their right to say "no" to an adult if they feel afraid or uncomfortable. Children must be taught to recognize appropriate and inappropriate touching.

On a community level, parents must inform themselves on issues of child abuse prevention. They must request that the subject be discussed at local community gatherings, parent and teacher school meetings, and in their churches. Parents should also write or phone government representatives on the need for public funding to establish child abuse prevention programs and victim-assisted services for both adults and children.

Lastly, parents must be mindful of the consequences when choosing appropriate measures to discipline children. If there is any doubt in the parents' mind as to what discipline practice they use, they should seek professional advice and counseling.

Recently, media attention has focused on priests, and members of religious groups who molest children. Is this surge of attention due to the occurrence of more victimizations or because more legal action has been filed against religious institutions?

I don't feel it is because more victimizations are being perpetrated now. Courageous survivors have decided to speak out and fight the church hierarchy for ignoring, concealing and protecting pedophilic men among their ministers. We have here another instance of family denial and avoidance of the subject of child sexual molestation. In this case the "family" is the Roman Catholic Church. Within the church, the issue of pedophilic priests has

long been viewed as a moral and psychological problem; one that can be corrected with extended periods of rest, retreats and spiritual counseling. The Church has been determined to work things out within its own structure, and therefore, has not retained the assistance of outside professional resources. It appears that the Church has only recently begun to view this problem as a serious economic crisis, due to the estimated $400 million it has, to date, paid out in legal fees to resolve pedophile priests abuse cases. It is projected that $1 billion may be paid by this century's end. Hopefully, the church will respond to the seriousness of this mental health crisis. Truly, it must not be overshadowed by the financial burden of endless lawsuits which the church has been engaged in.

This area of ministers and priests molesting members of their congregation is one that requires immediate attention. We can't imagine how many victims of clergy sexual abuse are out there in our communities. I only know that a tremendous amount of education, action and healing needs to take place between the leaders of the church, their ministers and their congregations. Children have always been susceptible to sexual molestation by clergy, but it is only recently that so many have come forward to confront the church on its irresponsible policies of protecting pedophilic clergy. For example, secret reassignments are a common method used to protect these individuals and their crimes. Parishes unknowingly receiving the new reassigned priests into their congregations, without warning of his abuse history, thus become the most likely candidates for victimization.

In your opinion, is there anything that religious congregations can do to prevent further sexual abuse by their clergy? How can these members protect themselves and their children?

I believe that the clergy and other leaders of religious congregations must begin to open themselves to the discussion of sexual abuse, pedophilia, adult survivor issues and prevention strategies. They must actively seek out professionals in the field, from outside their immediate circle of associates, and provide workshops, lectures, and educational programs for members of the clergy and the congregations. Those members of the clergy with known histories of pedophilia MUST BE PERMANENTLY REMOVED from ministries that may provide any potential opportunity for victimizing children, and not be reassigned to another ministry where contact with children is inevitable.

Congregations should insist that their church begin education, prevention and intervention programs. Children need to be taught the difference between appropriate and inappropriate touch, no matter who is doing the touching. They must be encouraged to foster their own sense of self-respect at a young age by not allowing anyone to violate their bodies. Further, if a violation occurs, the child needs to be taught that telling others immediately is the first step towards getting the abuse stopped.

Appropriately trained religious leaders, together with qualified sex abuse professionals, must facilitate community discussions on child sexual abuse prevention for both clergy and non-clergy. Foremost and not to be overlooked is to include the topic of sexual victimization by clergy. Simply avoiding the topic will only increase the odds of it happening.

If church authorities and representatives were to initiate honest dialogues about child sexual abuse with their congregations, I firmly believe that, those clergy currently molesting children would stop for fear of being exposed. Secondly, parishioners would be better prepared to report suspicious or alleged incidents of clergy sexual behavior to both civil and religious authorities. Thirdly, immediate and appropriate action can be taken to get professional counseling for the victim, as well as for the perpetrator.

Once again, the focus here is on male ministers and priest molesting children. Are there women religious/ministers who also sexually abuse children?

I have no doubt about it. Women do perpetrate sex crimes upon children, and being a nun or minister does not exclude one from committing the crime. However, here again we are faced with a prejudice: when women are involved with boys, the boys are not perceived as being victims of abuse. When the offender is a person in religious life, particularly a women, it becomes nearly impossible to tell because of its unthinkable and unbelievable magnitude. I am aware of several men who, when they were boys, had sexual molestation experiences with both nuns and female ministers. No profession, no matter how sacred it may appear, is immune from the problem of a pedophilic person acting out their sexual interest.

Hank, how is your life today?

Today, I've learned how to trust, respect and love myself and another person. I am also very much encouraged by the calls and letters that I receive from men throughout the country who seek to recover from similar childhood experiences.

With each passing day, I've noticed that I have learned to accommodate the pain and anger I experienced as a child, as being in its' rightful place, IN THE PAST. The memories don't leave, and I can't forget them, but that's all right. I slayed my dragon and realize that I'm now in the process of burying the negative remains. I know that recovery is possible and that all the wounds of the past will heal eventually.

Now that you've openly described and related your childhood ordeal, what's next.

I'll continue to speak out against child molestation and abuse on behalf of those of us who have experienced first-hand the brutal realities of our victimizations, and yet have not become abusers in our adult lives.

I will work to help other male victims speak out about their own childhood traumas. I will offer support and encouragement that will assist them with their healing and recovery. Finally, I urge others to break the silence and secrecy that, in my opinion, guarantees the continuation of child abuse behavior upon the next generation.

Bibliography
*Male Victimization

BOOKS (1970-1979)

Besharov, Douglas. **Child Sexual Abuse: Incest, Assault and Sexual Exploitation.** Washington, D.C.: U.S. Dept. of HEW, 1978.

Bohan, David. **Slaughter Of The Innocents.** Boston: Beacon Press, 1971.

Brady, Katherine. **Father's Day: A True Story of Incest.** New York: Seaview Brooks, 1979.

Burgess, Ann, Nicholas Groth, Lynda Holmstrom and Suzanne Sgroi. **Sexual Assault Of Children And Adolescents.** Lexington, MA.: Lexington Books, 1978.

Butler, Sandra. **Conspiracy Of Silence: The Trauma Of Incest.** San Francisco, CA.: New Clide Publications, 1978 and New York: Bantam Books.

Child Abuse And Neglect: The Family And The Community. Edited by R.E. Helfer and G.H. Kempe. Cambridge, MA.: Ballinger, 1976.

Copeland, L., et al. **Sexual Abuse Of Children.** San Francisco, CA.: Queens Bench Foundation, 1976.

DeFrancis, V. "Protecting The Abused Child: A Coordinated Approach." Pamphlet. Nat. Symposium on Child Abuse. Denver, CO.: Am. Humane Society, 1972.

Durkheim, E. Incest: **The Nature And Origin Of The Taboo.** New York: Lyle Stuart, 1973.

Evans, H.I., and N.B. Sperekas. **Sexual Assault Bibliography 1920-1975.** Catalog Of Selected Documents In Psychology, 1976.

Family Violence: An International Interdisciplinary Study. Edited by John M. Ekelaar and Sanford N. Katz. Toronto, Canada: Butterworth, 1978.

Fay, Jennifer. **He Told Me Not To Tell.** Renton, WA.: King Co. Rape Relief, 1979.

Finkelhor, David. **Sexually Victimized Children.** New York: Free Press, 1979.

Floyd, Robin. **Obscene But Not Forgotten.** Howard McCann, 1979.

Fontana, Vincent. **Somewhere A Child Is Crying.** New York: MacMillan Publishers, 1976.

Forward, Susan and Craig Breck. **Betrayal Of Innocence-Incest And Its Devastation.** New York: Penguin Books, 1978.

Geisen, Robert L. **Hidden Victims: The Sexual Abuse Of Children.** Boston, MA: Beacon Press, 1979.

Hunt, Morton. **Sexual Behavior In The 1970's.** New York: Dell, 1974.

Incest: In Search Of Understanding. Edited by Nahmon Greenberg, M.D., Washington, D.C.: Nat. Center On Child Abuse And Neglect, HEW, 1979.

Inglis, Ruth Langdon, **Sins Of The Fathers: A Study Of The Physical And Emotional Abuse Of Children.** New York: St. Martins Press, 1978.

Justice, Blair, and Rita Justice. **The Broken Taboo-Sex In The Family.** New York: Human Services Press, 1979.

Kempe, Ruth S. and C. Henry. **Child Abuse.** Cambridge, MA.: Harvard University Press, 1978.

Maisch, Herbert. **Incest.** New York: Stein & Day, 1972.

Masters, R.E.L. **Patterns of Incest.** New York: Julian Press, 1963, and New York: Ace Books, 1970.

Mathis, James L. **Clear Thinking About Sexual Deviation.** Chicago: Nelson-Hall Co., 1972.

Meiselman, Karin C. Incest: **A Psychological Study Of Causes And Effects With Treatment Recommendation.** San Francisco: Jossey-Bass, 1978.

Myers, Barbara. **Incest-If You Think The Word Is Ugly, Take A Look At Its Effects.** Minneapolis, MN.: Christopher Street, Inc., 1979.

Pincus, Lilly, and Christopher Dare. **Secrets In The Family.** New York: Harper & Row, 1978.

Robin, Floyd. **Boy Prostitution In America-For Money Or Love.** Vanguard, 1976.

Santiago, Lucieno. **The Children Of Oedipus: Borther & Sister Incest In Psychiatry, Literature. History And Mythology.** Libra, 1973.

Sexual Behaviors: Social, Clinical And Legal Aspects. Edited by H.L.P. Resnick and M.E. Wolfgang. Boston: Little, Brown & Co., 1972.

Sexual Encounters Between Adults And Children. Pamphlet by SIECUS. New York: Sex Information and Educational Council of U.S., 1970.

Sexual Offenses. Report by the Law Reform Commission of Canada. Ottowa: Ministry Of Supply And Services, 1978 (Catalog #J31-28.1978).

Stein, Robert. **Incest And Human Love: Betrayal Of The Soul In Psychotherapy.** New York: Third Press, 1973.

The Forbidden Love: The Normal And Abnormal Love Of Children. Edited by William Kraemer. London: Sheldon Press, 1976.

The Sexual Oppressed. Edited by Harvey and Jean Gochros. New York: Association Press, 1977.

Walters, David R. **Physical and Sexual Abuse Of Children: Causes And Treatment.** Bloomington, IN.: Indiana University Press, 1975.

Weinberg, Lirson. **Incest Behavior.** New York: Citadel Press, 1976.

Woodbury, John, and Elroy Schwartz. **The Silent Sin: A Case History Of Incest.** New York: New American Library & Signet Books, 1971.

PERIODICALS (1970-1979)

Anderson, Deborah. "Touching: When Is It Caring And Nurturing Or When Is It Exploitative And Damaging?" **Child Abuse And Neglect,** 3 (1979), pp. 793-794.

Anderson, Lorne, and Gretchen Schafer. "The Character-Disordered Family: A Community RX Model For Family Sexual Abuse." **American Journal Of Orthopsychiatry,** 49 (3) (July 1979), pp. 436-445.

Angel, Sherry. "Don't Be Afraid To Say 'No'!" **Redbook,** (July 1978), p. 40.

Armstrong, Louise. "Sex In The Family." **SIECCAN Newsletter,** 14 (December 1979).

Awad, G. "Father-Son Incest." **Journal of Nervous And Mental Disease**, 162 (1976), pp. 135-139.

Benwood, J., and J. Densen-Gerber. "Incest As A Causative Factor In Antisocial Behavior: An Exploratory Study." **Contemporary Drug Problems**, 4 (Fall 1975), p. 323.

Berliner, L. "Child Sexual Abuse: What Happens Next?" **Victimology**, 2 (Summer 1977), pp. 327-331.

Berry, Gail W. "Incest: Some Clinical Variations On A Classical Theme." **Journal Of The American Academy Of Psychoanalysis**, 3 (April 1975), pp. 151-162.

Blumberg, Marcia. "Child Sexual Abuse: Ultimate In Maltreatment Syndrome." **New York State Journal Of Medicine**, 78 No. 4 (1978), pp. 612-616.

Brant, Renee S. and Veronica Tisza. "The Sexually Misused Child." **American Journal Of Psychiatry**, 134 (January 1977) pp. 69-72.

Burgess, Ann, and Lynda Holmstrom. "Sexual Trauma Of Children And Adolescents: Pressure, Sex And Secrecy." **Nursing Clinics Of North America**, 10, No. 3 (September 1975) pp. 551-563.

DeFrancis, V. "Protecting The Child Victim Of Sex Crimes Committed By Adults." **Federal Probation**, 35 (September 1971), pp. 15-20.

DeMause, Floyd, "Our Forebears Made Childhood A Nightmare." **Psychology Today**, 8 (April 1975), pp. 85-88.

Dixon, K.N., L.E. Arnold, and K. Calestor. "Father-Son Incest: Unreported Psychiatric Problem?" **American Journal of Psychiatry**, 135 (July 1978), pp. 835-838.

Elwell, Mary E. "Sexually Assaulted Children And Their Families." **Social Casework**, 60 (April 1979), pp. 227-235.

Finch, S.M. "Adult Seduction Of The Child: Effects." **Medical Aspects Of Human Sexuality**, 7 (1973).

Finkelhor, David. "Psychological, Cultural And Family Factors In Incest And Family Sexual Abuse." **Journal Of Marital And Family Therapy**, 4 (October 1978), pp. 41-19.

Galdstone, Richard. "Sexual Survey #12: Current Thinking On Sexual Abuse Of Children." **Medical Aspects of Human Sexuality**, 12 (July 1978) p. 44.

"Incest: Hidden Menace." **Family Health,** 10 (August 1978), p. 16.

James, Jennifer. "Early Sexual Experiences And Prostitution." **American Journal Of Psychiatry,** No. 12 (1977), p. 134.

Jorne, Slager, Paula. "Counseling Sexually Abused Children." **Personnel And Journal,** 57 (October 1978), pp. 103-105.

Kates, Marcy. "Incest: The Taboo Next Door." **San Francisco,** 17 (February 1975), p. 24.

Kempe, Henry. "Sexual Abuse: Another Hidden Pediatric Problem." **Pediatrics,** 62 (September 1978), pp. 382-389.

Kirsch, T.B. "Incest And Human Love." **Journal Of Analytical Psychology,** 20 (July 1975), p. 237.

Kroth, Jerome A. "Family Therapy Impact On The Intrafamilial Child Sexual Abuse." **Child Abuse And Neglect,** 3, No. 1, (1979), pp. 297-302.

Lester, D. "Incest." **Journal Of Sex Research,** 8, No. 4 (November 1972), pp. 268-285.

Masters, W., and V. Johnson. "Incest: The Ultimate Sexual Taboo." **Redbook,** (April 1976).

Newton, David E. "Homosexual Behavior And Child Molestation: A Review Of The Evidence." **Adolescence,** 13 (1978), pp. 29-43.

Nichtern, Sol. "Effect Of Sexual Disturbances On Family Life." **Medical Aspects Of Human Sexuality,** 11, No. 3 (1977).

Paulson, Morris J. "Incest And Sexual Molestation: Children And Legal Issues." **Journal Of Clinical Child Psychology,** 7, (August 1978), pp. 177-180.

Quinsley, Vernon L., Terry Chaplin, and Wayne Carrigan. "Sexual Preference Among Incestuous And Non-Incestuous Child Molesters." **Behavior Therapy,** 14, No. 10 (September 1979), pp. 562-565.

Raphline, David L., Bob L. Carpenter, and David Allen. "Incest: A Genealogical Study." **Archives Of General Psychiatry,** 6, (April 1976), p. 505.

Renshaw. "Healing The Incest Wound." **Sexual Medicine Today,** (October 1977).

Rodolfa, Emil R. "A Bibliography On Child Sexual Abuse And Incest." **Catalog Of Selected Documents In Psychology,** 9, No. 55, (August 1979).

Sagarin, Edward. "Incest: Problems Of Definition And Frequency." **Journal Of Sex Research**, 13, No. 126 (May 1977).

Schultz, Leroy G. "The Sexual Abuse Of Children And Minors: A Bibliography." **Child Welfare**, 53 (March 1979), pp. 147-163.

Summit, Roland, and Ho-Ami Kryson. "Sexual Abuse Of Children: A Clinical Spectrum." **American Journal Of Orthopsychiatry**, 48, No. 2 (April 1978), p. 237.

"The Crime Of Incest Against The Minor Child And The States' Statutory Responses." **Journal Of Family Law**, 17, (November 1978), pp. 93-116.

Virkkunen, M. "Incest Offences And Alcoholism." **Medicine, Science And The Law**, 14, (1974), pp. 124-128.

BOOKS (1980-1993)

Adams, Caren, and Jennifer Fay. **No More Secrets: Protecting Your Child From Sexual Assault.** San Luis Obispo, CA.: Impact Publishers, 1981.

Adams, Caren, et al. **No Is Not Enough: Helping Teenagers Avoid Sexual Exploitation.** San Luis Obispo, CA.: Impact Publishers, 1984.

American Bar Association. **Innovations In The Prosecution Of Child Sexual Abuse Cases.** Washington, D.C.: Nat. Legal Resource Center For Child Advocacy & Protection, 1981.

Amstuty, Beverly. **Touch Me Not!** Illustrated Book Teaches Children To Be Aware Of Child Molesters. (Pamphlet) Precious Resources, Box 14463, Parkville, MO., 64252.

*Anderson, Arnold (Ed.). (1990). **Males with Eating Disorders.** New York: Bruner / Mazel.

Anderson, C. **Homosexuality And Psychotherapy.** Males As Sexual Assault Victims: Multiple Levels Of Trauma.

Anderson, Shirley Cook & Stephens. **Evaluation Of The Sexual Assault Patient In The Health Care System: A Medical Training Manual.** Seattle, WA.: University Of Washington, 1982.

Asher, Sandy. **Things Are Seldom What They Seem.** New York: Delacorte Press, 1983.

*Banning, Ann. (1989). "**Mother-Son Incest: Confronting A Prejudice,**" **Child Abuse & Neglect,** (13 (4), 563-570.

Barbach, L. **For Each Other: Sharing Sexual Intimacy.** New York: New American Library, 1982.

*Bear, Euan and Peter T. Dimock. **Adults Molested As Children: A Survivor's Manual For Women And Men.** Orwell, VT.: The Safer Society Press, 1988.

Benedict, H. **Recovery.** Garden City, NY: Doubleday, 1985.

*Berendzen, Richard. **Come Here: A Man Overcomes The Tragic Aftermath Of Childhood Sexual Abuse.** New York: Villard Books, 1993.

*Black, Stephen D. Grubman. **Broken Boys / Mending Men, Recovery From Childhood Sexual Abuse.** TAB Books, 1990.

*Bolton, F., Morris, L, MacEachron, A. **Males At Risk: The Other Side Of Child Sexual Abuse.** Newburry Park, CA: Sage, 1989.

Bradshaw, John. **Homecoming: Reclaiming and Championing Your Inner Child.** New York, Bantam, 1990.

Bradshaw, John. **Healing The Shame That Binds You.** Deerfield Beach, FL: Health Communications, Inc., 1988.

Brown, Evelyn, F. Berliner, and R. Raymond. Child Sexual Abuse Investigation: A Curriculum For Training Law Enforcement Officers. Seattle, WA.: Sexual Assault Center, Harborview Medical Center.

Burket, Elinor, Frank Bruni. A Gospel of Shame: Child Sexual Abuse And The Catholic Church. New York, Penguin Books, 1993.

Carnes, P. **Contrary To Love,** Minneapolis: Compcare, 1989.

Carnes, P. **Out Of The Shadows: Understanding Sexual Addiction.** Minneapolis: Compcare, 1983.

Carnes, P. **The Sexual Addiction.** Minneapolis: Compcare, 1983.

Caruso, Beverly. **Healing: A Handbook For Adult Victims Of Child Sexual Abuse.** 1986.

Child Sexual Abuse And The Law. Edited By Josephine Bulkey. Washington, D.C.: American Bar Association, 1981.

Colao, Flora and Tamer Hosansky. **Your Children Should Know: Teach Your Children The Strategies That Will Keep Them Safe From Assault And Crime.** Indianapolis, IN.: Bobbs-Merrill, 1983.

Crewdson, J. **By Silence Betrayed: Sexual Abuse Of Children In America.** Boston: Little, Brown, 1988.

Cudney, Milton R. and Robert E. Hardy. **Self-Defeating Behaviors.** New York, Harper Collins. 1992.

Cuyler, Cathy. **Safety Tips (Sexual Abuse: Facts And Education For Today's Youth And Teen Incest Prevention Suggestions.** Columbus, OH.: Issue, Inc., 1984.

Davis, James R. **Help Me, I'm Hurt, The Child Abuse Handbook.** Dubuque, IO.: Kendall Hunt Pub. Co., 1982.

Davis, L. **Allies In Healing.** New York: Harper/Collins, 1991.

Davis, L. **Beginning To Heal.** New York: Harper & Row.

*Davis, L. **The Courage To Heal Workbook.** New York: Harper & Row, 1990.

DeYoung, Mary. **The Sexual Victimization Of Children.** Jefferson, N.C.: McFarland, 1982.

*Estrada, Hank. **Recovery For Male Victims Of Child Sexual Abuse.** Santa Fe, NM: Red Rabbit Press, 1994.

Eth, Spencer & Pynoos, Robert. **Post-Traumatic Stress Disorders In Children.** Washington, D.C.: American Psychiatric Press, 1985.

Erickson, Edsel L., Alan W. McEvoy and Nicholas D. Colucci Jr. **Child Abuse And Negligence: A Guidebook For Educators And Community Leaders.** Kalamazoo, MI.: Learning Publications.

Faller, K.C. **Understanding Child Sexual Maltreatment.** Newbury Park, CA. SAGE. 1990.

Families, Incest And Therapy. Edited by Charles P. Barnard. (Special Issue 1JFT Ser: Vol. 5, No. 2), Human Science Press, 1983, p. 92.

Farmer, Steven. **Adult Children Of Abusive Parents.** Lowell House, 1989.

Finkelhor, D. **Child Sexual Abuse: New Theory & Research.** New York: The Free Press, 1984.

Finkelhor, D. **Sexually Victimized Children.** New York: The Free Press, 1979.

Finkelhor, D. **Sourcebook On Child Sexual Abuse.** Beverly Hills, CA: Sage Publications, 1986.

Fong, Pamela. **Breaking the Cycle: Survivors of Child Abuse and Neglect.** Norton, 1991.

Fox, Robin. **The Red Lamp Of Incest: What The Taboo Can Tell Us About Who We Are And How We Got That Way.** Dutton, 1980.

Gannon, Patrick. **Soul Survivors: A New Beginning For Adults Abused As Children.** P.H., 1989.

Garlearino, James and Gwen Gillion. **Understanding Abusive Families.** Lexington, MA.: Lexington Books, 1980.

Giaretto, Henry. **Integrated Treatment Of Child Sexual Abuse.** Palo Alto, CA.: Science & Behavior Books, 1982.

Gil, Eliana. **Outgrowing The Pain,** San Francisco, CA.: Launch Press, 1984.

Gil, Eliana. **Treatment Of Adult Survivors Of Childhood Abuse.** San Francisco, CA.: Launch Press, 1988.

Goodwin, Jean. **Sexual Abuse Incest Victims And Their Families.** Boston: John Wright, 1982.

Graber, Ken. **Ghosts in the Bedroom: A Guide For Partners Of Incest Survivors.** 1991.

Greven, Phillip. **Spare The Child: The Religious Roots Of Punishment: The Psychological Impact Of Physical Abuse.** Random. 1992.

*Grubman, Black, Stephen. **Broken Boys-Mending Men: Recovery From Childhood Sexual Abuse.** Ivy Books, 1992.

Heitritter, R.N, **Helping Victims Of Sexual Abuse.** Bethany House, 1989.

Helfer, Ray E. **Childhood Comes First-A Crash Course In Childhood For Adults.** East Lansing, MI.: Ray E. Helfer, 1984.

Hobbs, Bobbi. **Secrets: Therapy For Adults Molested As Children.** Windrose Pubs., 1988.

*Hunter, Mic. **Abused Boys: The Neglected Victims Of Sexual Abuse.** Lexington, MA.: Lexington Books, 1989.

Hunter, Mic & Jem. **The First Step For People In Relationships With Sex Addicts: A Workbook For Recovery.** Minneapolis, MN: Compcare Publishers, 1990.

Hyde, Margaret. **Cry Softly!: The Story Of Child Abuse.** Philadelphia: Westminster Press, 1980.

Inger, Benjamin. **Sexual Abuse Of Children: A Resource Guide And Annotated Bibliography.** Toronto, Ontario, Canada: University of Toronto Press, 1982.

James, Beverly and Naria Nasjleti. **Consulting Psychology.** "Treating Sexually Abused Children And Their Families." 1983.

Kane, Evangeline. **Recovering From Incest: Imagination And The Healing Process.** 1989.

Kaplan, H.W. **The Evaluation Of Sexual Disorders.** New York: Brunner Mazel, 1983.

Kaufman, Arthur. **Victims Of Sexual Aggression: Treatment Of Children, Women, and Men.** Rape Of Men In The Community. In I.R. Stuart & J.G. Greer (Eds.), New York: Van Nostrand Reinhold, 1982.

Keen, Sam. **Fire In The Belly: On Being A Man.** New York, Bantam, 1991.

Kempe, Ruth S. and C. Henry. **The Common Secret: Sexual Abuse Of Children And Adolescents.** New York: W.H. Freeman & Co., 1984.

Killman, P.R., and Mills, K.H. **All About Sex Therapy.** New York: Plenum Press, 1983.

*Lee, John. (1987). **The Flying boy: Healing The Wounded Man.** Deerfield Beach, FL.: Health Communications, Inc.

*Lew, Mike. **Victims No Longer: Men Recovering From Incest And Other Sexual Child Abuse.** New York: Harper & Row, 1990.

Lieblum, S., Pervin, L. **Principles And Practices Of Sex Therapy.** New York: Plenum Press, 1980.

Lieblum, S.R., Rosen, R.C. **Sexual Desire Disorders.** New York: Guilford Press, 1988.

Linedecher, Clifford. **Children In Chains.** New York: Everest House, 1981.

Maltz, W., Holman, B. **Incest And Sexuality: A Guide To Understanding And Healing.** Lexington, MA: D.C. Health & Co., 1987.

Maltz, W. **The Sexual Healing Journey: A Guide For Survivors Of Sexual Abuse.** New York: Harper Collins, 1991.

Mayer, Adele. **Incest: A Treatment Manual For Therapy With Victims, Spouses And Offenders.** Learning Publications, 1982.

Mayer, Adele. **Sexual Abuse: A Guide For Those Working With Children And Adolescents.** Learning Publications, 1984.

McCann, Lisa and Laurie Pearlman. **Psychological Trauma & The Adult Survivor: Theory, Therapy & Transformation.** 1990.

Miller, Alice. **For Your Own Good: Hidden Cruelty In Childrearing & The Roots Of Violence.** New York: Farrar & Straus, 1983.

Miller, Alice. **Thou Shalt Not Be Aware: Society's Betrayal Of The Child.** New York: New American Library, 1984.

Mura, David. **A Male Grief: Notes On Pornography & Addiction.** Minneapolis: Milkweed Editions, 1987.

Mrazek, Patricia B. and Kempe, C.H. **Sexually Abused Children And Their Families.** Pergamon, 1982.

Nelson, Mary and Clark, Kay, Eds. **The Educator's Guide To Preventing Child Sexual Abuse.** Network Pubns, 1986.

Nelson, S. **Incest: Fact And Myth.** Edinburgh: Stramullion, Cooperative, Ltd., 1982.

O'Brian, Shirley. **Child Abuse, A Crying Shame.** Provo, Utah: Bringham Young University Press, 1980.

*Porter, Eugene. **Treating The Young Male Victim Of Sexual Assault: Issues And Intervention Strategies.** New York: Safer Society Press, 1988.

Ratner, Ellen. **The Other Side Of The Family-A Book For Recovery From Abuse, Incest And Neglect.** Health Communications, Inc., 1990.

Reich, Wilhelm. **Children Of The Future: On The Prevention Of Sexual Pathology.** 1984.

Rencken, R.H. **Intervention Strategies For Sexual Abuse.** Alexandria, VA Am Association for Counseling and Development, 1989.

Renshaw, Domeena. **Incest: Understanding And Treatment.** Little, Brown and Little, 1982.

Revoize, Jean. **Incest: A Family Pattern.** London: Routledge and Kegan Paul, 1982.

Rogers, C.M. & Terry, T. **Victims Of Sexual Aggression: Treatment Of Children, Women & Men.** New York: Van Nostrand Reinhold, 1984.

Rush, Florence. **The Best Kept Secret-Sexual Abuse Of Children.** New York: McGraw Hill, 1981.

Sanford, Linda Tschirhart. **The Silent Children: A Guide To The Prevention Of Child Sexual Abuse.** Garden City, N.Y.: Anchor Press/Doubleday, 1980, and New York: McGraw Hill, 1982.

Sanford, Linda T. **Strong At The Broken Places: Overcoming The Trauma Of Childhood Abuse.** Avon, 1992.

Sanford, Paula. **Healing Victims Of Sexual Abuse.** Victory House, 1988.

Sexual Abuse of Children: Selected Readings. Edited by B.M. Jones, L.L. Jenstrom and L. MacFarlone. Washington, D.C.: Nat. Center On Child Abuse and Neglect, HEW, 1980.

Sexually Abused Children And Their Families. Edited by Patricia Beezley Mrazek and C. Henry Kempe. Oxford, N.Y.: Pergamon Press, 1981.

Sgroi, Suzanne M. **Handbook of Clinical Interventions In Child Sexual Abuse.** Lexington Books, 1981.

Shengold Leonard. **Soul Murder: The Effects Of Childhood Abuse And Deprivation.** New Haven: Yale University, 1989.

Shepher, Joseph. **Incest: A Bio Social View.** Garland Publishers, 1981.

*Sonkin, Daniel Jay. **Wounded Men: Healing From Childhood Abuse.** New York: Harper & Row, 1988.

Stark, Evan. **Everything You Need To Know About Sexual Abuse.** Rosen Group, 1988.

Stordeur, R.A. and R. Stillie. **Ending Men's Violence Against Their Parents: One Road To Peace.** Newbury Park, CA. Sage, 1989.

Straus, M., Gelles, R., & Steinmetz, S. **Behind Closed Doors: Violence In The American Family.** Newbury Park, CA: Sage, 1988.

*Thomas, T. **Men Surviving Incest: A Male Survivor Shares The Process Of Recovery.** Walnut Creek, CA: Launch Press, 1989.

Thomas, T. **Surviving With Serenity: Daily Meditations For Incest Survivors.** Deerfield Beach, FL: Health Communications, 1990.

Thorman, George. **Incestuous Families.** Springfield, IL: Garland Publishers, 1981.

Van der Kolk, Bessel. **Psychological Trauma.** Washington, D.C.: American Psychiatric Press, 1987.

W. Nancy. **On The Path: Affirmations For Adults Suffering From Childhood Sexual Abuse.** San Francisco, CA. Harper, 1991.

Wachter, Oralee. **No More Secrets For Me.** Boston: Little, Brown and Co., 1983.

Webster, Linda, ed. **Sexual Assault And Child Sexual Abuse: A National Directory of Victim Services And Prevention Programs.** Oryx Pr., 1989.

Wiehe, V.R. **Sibling Abuse: Hidden Physical, Emotional, And Sexual Trauma.** Lexington, MA. Lexington Books, 1990.

Wyatt, Gail E., & Powell, Gloria J. (ed.). **Lasting Effects Of Child Sexual Abuse.** Newbury Park, CA. Sage Publications, 1988.

PERIODICALS (1980-1992)

"Abusing Common Sense". National Review, 42:16-17, (May 28, 1990).

Adams-Tucker, C. "Proximate Effects Of Sexual Abuse In Childhood: A Report On 28 Children." **American Journal Of Psychiatry,** 139 (October 1982), pp. 1252-6.

Alexander, P.C. "Family Characteristics And Long-Term Consequences Associated With Sex Abuse." **Arc. sex** behavior, 16: (June 1987), p. 235.

Andrews, D.D. and R.R. Linden. "Preventing Rural Child Abuse: Progress In Spite Of Cutbacks." **Child Welfare,** S / O 1984, pp. 443-452.

Astrachan, A. and B. Freer. "Incest Survivors Who Sue." **Glamour,** 86:74 (January 1988).

Barbee, H.E., Butt, J., & Marshall, W.L. "Sexual Offenders Against Male Children: Sexual Preferences." **Behavior Research & Therapy,** 26 (5), (1988), pp. 645-649.

Barry, B.J. "Incest: The Last Taboo." **FBI Law Enforcement Bulletin,** 53 (January 1984), pp. 2-9 and 53, (February 1984), pp. 15-19.

Bergart, A.M. "Isolation To Intimacy: Incest Survivors In Group Therapy." **Social Casework,** (May 1986), pp. 266-75.

Besharou, D.J. "Child Abuse And Neglect: Liability For Failing To Report." **Trial,** 22 (August 1986), pp. 67-68.

*Bidwell, R.J., Deisher, R.W., "Sexual Abuse Of Male Adolescents." **Seminars In Adolescent Medicine,** 3(1), (1987), pp. 47-54.

Bixler, R.H. "Mechanism For Avoidance Of Incest." **Psychological Reports,** 48 (June 1981), pp. 978-979.

Bixler, R.H. "The Incest Controversy." **Psychological Reports,** 49 (August 1981), pp. 267-283.

*Blanchard, G. "Male Victims Of Child Sexual Abuse: A Portent Of Things To Come." **Journal Of Independent Social Work,** 1 (1), (1986), pp. 19-27.

*Blanchard, Geral. (1986). **"Sexual Molestation of Boys: Identification & Treatment,"** Protecting Children. Fall. 22-23.

Bradshaw, J. "Incest: When You Wonder If It Happened To You." **Lear's,** 5:43-4 (August 92).

"Breaking The Incest Taboo: Those Who Crusade For Family Love Forget The Balance Of Family Power." **Progressive**, (May 1981), p. 16.

*Briere, J., Evans, D., Runtz, M. & Wall, T. "Symptomatology In Men Who Were Molested As Children: A Comparison Study." **American Journal Of Orthopsychiatry**, 58, (1988), pp. 457-461.

*Briere, J.N. "Molested Victims Pain Persists." **USA Today**, (August 90).

Briere, J., Evans, D., Runtz, M., & Wall, T. (1988). **"Symptomatology in Men Who Were Molested As Children: A Comparison Study,"** American Journal of Orthopsychiatry, 58, 457-461.

Browne, A., and D. Finkelhor. "Impact Of Child Sexual Abuse: A Review Of The Research." **Psychology Bulletin**, 99 (January 1986), pp. 66-77.

*Bruckner, D., and Johnson, P. "Treatment For Adult Male Victims Of Childhood Sexual Abuse." Social Cassework: **The Journal Of Contemporary Social Work**, 68 (2), (1987), pp. 81-87.

Burgess, A.W., Hartman, C.R., McCausland, M.P., and Powers, P. "Response Patterns In Children And Adolescents Exploited Through Sex Rings And Pornography." **American Journal Of Psychiatry**, 141 (5), (1984), pp. 656-662.

Butler, S. "Incest: Whose Reality, Whose Theory." **Aegis**, Summer / Autumn 1980), pp. 48-55.

Byrne, J.P., and E.V. Valdiserri. "Victims Of Childhood Sexual Abuse: A Follow-Up Study Of A Noncomplaint Population." **Hospital And Community Psychiatry**, 33 (November 1982), pp. 938-939.

Cameron, P., and others. "Child Molestation And Homosexuality." **Psychology Report**, 58 (February 1986), pp. 327-337.

Campbell, B.M. "When Words Hurt (Parents Use Of Verbal Abuse)." **Essence**, 20: 88 (July 1989).

Chance, P. "The Divided Self." **Psychology Today**, 20 (September 1986), p. 72.

Chandler, Susan Meyers. "Knowns And Unknowns In Sexual Abuse Of Children." **Journal Of S.W. And Human Sexuality**, 1, No 1 & 2, (Fall, Winter 1983), pp. 51-69.

Connors C. "Priest And Pedophilia: A Silence That Needs Breaking?" **America**, (May 9, 1992).

Curtis, J.M. "Factors In Sexual Abuse Of Children." **Psychology Report,** 58 (April 1986), pp. 591-587.

Dean, A.L. and others. "Effects Of Parental Maltreatment On Children's Conceptions Of Interpersonal Relations." **Develop Psychology,** 22 (September 1986), pp. 617-626.

Deighton, J. and P. McPeek. "Group Treatment: Adult Victims Of Childhood Sexual Abuse." **Social Casework,** 66 (September 1985), pp. 403-410.

Dekker, Anthony H. "The Incidence Of Sexual Abuse In HIV Infected Adolescents And Young Adults." **Journal of Adolescent Health Care.** 11:263, (1990).

DeLong, A. "The Sexually Abused Child: A Comparison Of Male And Female Victims." **Child Abuse And Neglect,** 9(4), (1985), pp. 576-586.

DeLong, A., et al. "Epidemiologic Factors In The Sexual Abuse Of Boys." **American Journal Of Diseases In Children,** 134 (155), (1980).

Deykin, E.Y., and others. "A Pilot Study Of The Effect Of Exposure To Child Abuse Or Neglect On Adolescent Suicidal Behavior." **American Journal Of Psychiatry,** 142 (November, 1985), pp. 1299-1303.

DeYong, M. "Innocent Seducer Or Innocently Seduced: The Role Of The Child Incest Victim." **Journal Of Clinical Child Psychology,** 11 (Sprint 1982), pp. 56-60.

*Dimock, P.T. "Adult Males Sexually Abused As Children: Characteristics And Implications For Treatment." **Journal Of Interpersonal Violence,** 3(2), (1988), pp. 203-221.

Ellenson, G.S. "Detecting A History Of Incest: A Predictive Syndrome." **Social Casework,** 66 (November 1985), pp. 325-332.

*Ellerstein, M.S., and J.W. Conavan. "Sexual Abuse Of Boys." **American Journal Of Diseases Of Children,** 134 (March 1980), pp. 255-257.

Erickson, W.D., and others. "Behavior Patterns Of Child Molesters." **Archives Of Sex Behavior,** 17 (February 1988), pp. 77-86.

Faller, Kathleen C. "Characteristics Of A Clinical Sample Of Sexually Abused Children: How Boy And Girl Victims Differ." **Child Abuse And Neglect,** 13, (1989), pp. 281-291.

Farber, E., J. Showers, et al. "The Sexual Abuse Of Children: A Comparison Of Male & Female Victims." **Journal Of Clinical Child Psychology,** 13, (3), (1984), pp. 294-297.

Finkelhor, David. "Risk Factors In The Sexual Victimization Of Children." **Child Abuse And Neglect,** 4 (1980), pp. 265-273.

Finkelhor, David. "Sex Among Siblings: A Survey On Prevalence, Variety And Effects." **Archives Of Sexual Behavior,** 9 (June 1980), pp. 171-194.

*Finkelhor, David & Hotaling, Gerald. (1990). **"Sexual Abuse In A National Survey Of Adult Men & Women: Prevalence, Characteristics, & Risk Factors,"** Child Abuse & Neglect, 14, (1), 19-28.

Folkenberg, J. "When Shame Hides Pain (Treatment Of Post-Traumatic Stress Disorder In Sexual Abused Children)." **American Health,** (May 1991).

*Freeman-Longo, R.E. "The Impact Of Sexual Victimization Of Males." **Child Abuse & Neglect,** 10, (1986), pp. 411-416.

*Friedrich, W., Beilke, R., & Urquiza, A. "Behavior Problems In Young Sexually Abused Males." **Journal Of Interpersonal Violence,** 3(1), (1988), pp. 21-28.

*Friedrich, W., Beliner, L. Urquiza, A., & Beilke, R. "Brief Diagnostic Group Treatment Of Sexually Abused Boys." **Journal Of Interpersonal Violence,** 3(3), (1988), pp. 331-343.

*Fritz, G., Stoll, K. & Wagner, N. "A Comparison Of Males & Females Who Were Sexually Molested As Children." **Journal Of Sex & Marital Therapy,** 7(1), (1981), pp. 54-59.

*Fromuth, M.E. & Burkhart, B.R. "Long-Term Psychological Correlates Of Childhood Sexual Abuse In Two Samples Of College Men." **Child Abuse And Neglect,** 13, (1989), pp. 533-542.

Gilgun, J.F. "Factors Which Block The Development Of Sexually Abusive Behavior In Adults Abused And Neglected As Children (Revision)." Paper presented at the National Conference On Male Victims and Offenders, 1988.

*Gite, L. "When Boys Are Raped." **Essence,** 22:61-2, (November 91).

Gold, E. P. "Long-Term Effects Of Sexual Victimization In Childhood: An Attributional Approach." **Journal Consult Clin-Psycholo,** 54 (August 1986), pp. 471-475.

Gordy, P.L. "Group Work That Supports Adult Victims Of Child-hood Incest." **Social Casework,** 64 (May 1983), pp. 300-307.

Gorman, C. "Incest Comes Out Of The Dark." **Time,** 138:46-7 (October 7, 1991).

*Groth, A. Nicholas & Burgess, A. "Male Rape: Offenders & Victims." **American Journal Of Psychiatry,** 137, (7), (1980), pp. 806-810.

Gupta, G.R., and S.M. Cox. "A Typology Of Incest And Possible Intervention Strategies." **Journal Of Family Violence,** 3(4), (1988), pp. 299-312.

*Halpern, J. "Family Therapy In Father-Son Incest: A Case Study." **Social Casework: The Journal Of Contemporary Social Work,** 68(2), (1987), pp. 88-93.

Hawkin, W.E.,, and D.F. Duncan. "Perpetrator And Family Characteristics Related To Child Abuse And Neglect: Comparison Of Substantiated And Unsubstantiated Reports." **Psych. Report,** 56 (April 85), pp. 407-410.

Haynes-Seman, C., and R.D. Krugman. "Sexualized Attention: Normal Interaction Or Precurser To Sexual Abuse." **American Journal Of Orthopsychiatry,** 59(2), (1989), pp. 238-245.

Herman, J. "Long-Term Effects Of Incestuous Abuse In Childhood." **American Journal Psychiatry,** 144 (July 1987), pp. 967-968.

Hill, G.D., and M.P. Atkinson. "Gender, Familiar Control, and Delinquency." **Criminology,** 26 (F 1988), pp. 127-149.

Hoorwitz, A.N. "When To Intervene In Cases Of Suspected Incest." **Social Casework,** 63 (June 1982), pp. 374-375.

*Hunter, Mic (Ed). (1990), **The Sexually Abused Male, Vol. 1: Prevalence, Impact & Treatment.** Lexington, MA.: Lexington Books.

*Hunter, Mic (Ed.). (1990). **The Sexually Abused Male, Vol. 2: Application Of Treatment Strategies.** Lexington, MA.: Lexington Books.

Jackson, Thomas L., and William P. Ferguson. "Attribution Of Blame In Incest." **American Journal Of Community Psychology,** 11 (June 1983), pp. 313-322.

*Janus, M.D., Burgess, A.W., & McCormick, A. (1987). "Histories of Sexual Abuse in Adolescent Male Runaways," **Adolescence,** 22 (86), 405-417.

*Janus, M.D., and others. "Histories Of Sexual Abuse In Adolescent Male Runaways." **Adolescence**, 22 (Summer 1987), pp. 405-417.

*Johanek, M.F. "Treatment Of Male Victims Of Child Sexual Abuse In Military Service." In S.M. Sgroi (ED). **Vulnerable Populations**, Volume 2, (1988), pp. 103-113.

*Johnson, R., & Shrier, D. "Sexual Victimization Of Boys." **Journal Of Adolescent Health Care**, 6 (1985), pp. 372-376.

Karlsberg, E. "Incest: Breaking The Silence." **Teen**, 34 (October 1990).

Kaufman, J., and E. Zigler. "Do Abused Children Become Abusive Parents?" **American Journal Of Orthopsychiatry**, 57 (April 1987), pp. 186-192.

Keating, S.S. "Children In Incestuous Relationships: The Forgotten Victims." **Loyola Law Review**, 34 (1988), pp. 111-123.

Kimmel, M.S. "Searching For Father." **Psychology Today**, 20 (June 1986), p. 71.

Kocol, C. "Child Abuse And Society's Response." **The Humanist**, 48:39 (S/O 1988).

*Krug, R. "Adult Male Report Of Childhood Sexual Abuse By Mothers." **Child Abuse & Neglect**, 13, (1989) pp. 111-119.

Lamb, S. "Treating Sexually Abused Children: Issues Of Blame And Responsibility." **American Journal Orthopsychiatry**, 56 (April 1986), p. 303.

Lande, R.G. "Incest: It's Causes And Repercussions." **Postgraduate Medicine**, 85(8), (1989), pp. 81-92.

*Langsley, D., et. al. (1968). "Father-Son Incest", **Comprehensive Psychiatry**, 9 (3), May, 218-226.

*Lew, Mike. (Forthcoming). "Male Incest: Factors That Inhibit Disclosure & Obstruct Treatment of Men In Recovery From Child Sexual Abuse," **Victimology.**

Lee, S.Y. "If You Suspect You Were Abused." **McCall's**, (September 1991).

Loftus, J.A. "A Question Of Disillusionment: Sexual Abuse Among The Clergy." **America**, 426-9. (December 1, 1990).

Mann, M.B. "Victims Of Abuse: Paying The Price For The Sins Of Others, (Child Molestation And Catholic Teaching)." **U.S. Catholic**, 54:36-8, (July 1989).

*Margolin, L. (1986). "The Effects of Mother-Son Incest," **Lifestyles: A Journal of Changing Patterns.**

McCarthy, L.M. "Investigation Of Incest: Opportunity To Motivate Families To Seek Help." **Child Welfare,** 60 (December 1981), pp. 679-689.

McCarty, L. "Mother-Child Incest: Characteristics Of The Offender." **Child Welfare,** 65(5), (1986).

McLeer, S.V., E. Deblinger, M.S. Atkins, Foa, E.B. et al. "Post-Traumatic Stress Disorder In Sexually Abused Children." **Journal Of The American Academy Of Child And Adolescent Psychiatry,** 17(5), (1988), pp. 650-654.

*McMullen, Richie. (1990). **Male Rape: Breaking The Silence On The Last Taboo.** London, England: The Gay Men's Press.

Mead, J.M. and N.E. Mead. "Postmolestation Regression In Children." **American Journal Psychiatry,** 143 (April 1986), p. 559.

Meyer, W.S. "An Abused Child Grows Up And Enters Treatment." **Clinical Social Work,** 15 (Summer 1987), pp. 136-147.

*Miller, N. "Male Rape." **Boston Phoenix,** 12, (November 1983).

Milner, T.S. "Screening Spouse Abusers For Child Abuse Potential." **Journal Of Clinical Psychology,** 42 (January 1986), pp. 169-172.

Mithers, C.L. "Incest And The Law." **The New York Times Magazine,** p. 44, (October 21, 1990).

Mithers, C.L. "Sexual Compulsions: When Nice Men Have Secret Vices." **Ladies Home Journal,** 105:64 (June 1988).

*Montan, C., A.W. Burgess, C.A. Grant, and C.R. Hartman. "The Case Of Two Trials: Father-Son Incest." **Journal Of Family Violence,** 4(1) (1989), pp. 95-103.

Moss, P.J. "The Face Of Abuse." **Psychology Today,** 21 (July 1987), p. 20.

*Mura, David. (1987). **A Male Grief: Notes on Pornography & Addiction.** Minneapolis: Milkweed Editions.

*Myers, M.F. "Men Sexually Assaulted As Adults And Sexually Abused As Boys." **Archives Of Sexual Behavior,** 18(3) (1989) pp. 203-215.

*Nasjleti, Maria "Suffering In Silence: The Male Incest Victim." **Child Welfare,** 59 (May 1980), pp. 269-275.

*Neilson, T. "Sexual Abuse Of Boys: Current Perspectives." **Personnel And Guidance Journal,** 62, (3), (1983), 139-142.

O'Brian, R.M. "Exploring The Intersexual Nature Of Violent Crimes." **Criminology,** 26 (February 1988), pp. 1510-170.

*Peake, A. "Issues Of Under-Reporting: The Sexual Abuse Of Boys." **Educational & Child Psychology,** 6 (1), pp. 42-50.

*Pierce, L. "Father-Son Incest: Using The Literature To Guide Practice." **Social Casework: The Journal Of Contemporary Social Work,** 68, (2), (1987), pp. 67-74.

*Pierce R. & Pierce, L. (1985). "The Sexually Abused Child: A Comparison of Male & Female Victims", **Child Abuse and Neglect,** Vol. 9, 191-199.

Reiker, P.P., and E. (Hilberman) Carmen. "The Victim-To Patient Process: The Disconfirmation And Transformation Of Abuse." **American Journal Orthopsychiatry,** 56 (July 1986), pp. 360-370.

*Reinhart, M. "Sexually Abused Boys." **Child Abuse And Neglect,** 11, (1987), pp. 229-235.

*Risin, L., Kross, M. "The Sexual Abuse Of Boys: Prevalence & Descriptive Characteristics Of Childhood Victimizations." **Journal Of Interpersonal Violence,** 2(3), (1987), pp. 309-323.

*Rogers, C.M. & Terry, T. (1984) "Clinical Intervention With Boy Victims of Sexual Abuse", in I.R. Stuart & J.G. Greer (Eds.), **Victims of Sexual Aggression: Treatment of Children, Women & Men.** Von Nostrand Reinhold, NY.

Saltman, V., and R.S. Solomon. "Incest And The Multiple Personality." **Psychological Reports,** 50 (June 1982), pp. 1127-1141.

*Sarrel, P.M., Masters, W.H. "The Sexual Molestation Of Men By Women." **Archives Of Sexual Behavior,** 2, (1982), pp. 117-131.

*Sebold, J. "Indicators Of Child Sexual Abuse In Males." **Social Casework: The Journal Of Contemporary Social Work,** 68(2), (1987), pp. 75-80.

Seligman, J. "Emotional Child Abuse." **Newsweek,** 112:48 (October 1988).

Shapiro, J.P. "Whose Responsibility Is It Anyway? Child Welfare Worker Liability." **U.S. News And World Report,** 106:29 (January 1989).

*Showers, J., Farber, E., Joseph, J., Oshins, L., Johnson, C. "The Sexual Victimization Of Boys: A Three-Year Survey." **Health Values: Achieving High Level Wellness,** 7, (1983), pp. 15-18.

Silbert, M.H., Pines, A.M. "Child Sexual Abuse As An Antecedent To Prostitution." **Child Abuse And Neglect,** 5, (1981), pp. 407-411.

Silver, R.L., et al. "Searching For Meaning In Misfortune: Making Sense Of Incest. **Journal Science Issues,** 39 No.2 (1983), pp. 81-101.

Silverman, M.M. and others. "Control Of Stress And Violent Behavior: Mid-Course Review Of The 1990 Health Objectives." **Public Health Report,** 103 (January/February 1988), pp. 38-49.

*Singer, K.I. "Group Work With Men Who Experienced Incest In Childhood." **American Journal Of Orthopsychiatry,** 59 (3), (1989), pp. 468-472.

*Spencer, M., Dunkleee, P. "Sexual Abuse Of Boys." **Pediatrics,** 78 (1), (1986), pp. 133-138.

Spiegal, L.D. "Child Abuse Hysteria: A Warning For Educators." **The Education Digest,** 54:55 (January 1989).

*Struve, Jim. (1990). "Dancing With The Patriarchy: The Politics of Sexual Abuse," in Mic Hunter (Ed.) **The Sexually Abused Male, Vol. 1: Prevalence, Impact, & Treatment.** Lexington, MA: Lexington Books.

*Struve, J. "Treatment Of The Sexually Abused Male." **Ridgeview Insight,** 10(2), (1989), pp. 25-31.

Tavris, C. "Prisoners Of Childhood." **Vogue,** 179-380 (March 1989).

Tilelli, John A., Dionne Turek, and Arthur C. Jaffe. "Sexual Abuse Of Children: Clinical Findings And Implications For Management." **The New England Journal Of Medicine,** 302 (February 1980), pp. 319-323.

Toufexis, A. "Bisexuality: What Is It?" **Time,** 140 49-51, (August 17, 1992).

Toufexis, A. "What Is Incest?" **Time,** 140:57, (August 31, 1992).

Trotter, R.J. "Failing To Find The Father-Infant Bond." **Psychology Today,** 20 (February 1986), p. 18.

Tysoe, Maryon. "Self-Help For Incest Victims." **New Society,** 58 (October 1981), p. 199.

*Vander Mey, B.J. "The Sexual Victimization Of Male Children: A Review Of Previous Research." **Child Abuse And Neglect,** 12 (1988), pp. 61-72.

Vander Mey, B. J., Neff R. "Adult-Child Incest: A Review Of Research And Treatment." **Adolescence,** 17 (Winter 1982), pp. 717-735.

Vasques, M., Kitchener, K.S. "Ethics In Counseling: Sexual Intimacy Between Counselor And Client." **Journal Of Counseling & Development,** 67, (4), (1988), pp. 214-241.

"Violence Begets Violence." USA Today, 118:3, (December 1989).

Waller, P. "The Politics Of Child Abuse" bibl. **Society,** 28:6-13, (September 1991).

White, J. Blake, and C.M. Kline. "Treating The Dissociative Process In Adult Victims Of Childhood Incest." **Social Casework,** 66 (September 1985), pp. 394-402.

Widom, Cathy S. "Child Abuse: A Cycle Of Violence?" **Science News,** 136:61 (July 22, 1989).

*Williams, M. "Father-Son Incest: A Review And Analysis Of Reported Incidents." **Clinical Social Work Journal,** 16 (2), (1988), pp. 165-179.

Woodward, K.L. "The Sins Of The Father (Allegations Of Child Molestation Against Former Priests)." **Newsweek,** (June 1992).

*Zaphiris, Alexander. "The Sexually Abused Boy." **Preventing Sexual Abuse,** A Newsletter Of The National Family Life Education Network, 1(1), (1986), 1-4.

Zierler, Sally. "Adult Survivors Of Child Sexual Abuse And Subsequent Risk of HIV Infection." **American Journal of Public Health,** 81:572-75, (1991).

Zigler, E.F. "Do Abused Children Become Abusive Parents?" **Parents,** 63:100 (May 1988).

SELECTED READINGS ON OCCULT & RITUAL ABUSE (Before 1980)

Anatomy Of The Occult. Buckland, Raymond.

The Back Side Of Satan. Cerullo, Morris. Creation House, 1973. (Explores satanism from a Christian Viewpoint. Lists satanic related crimes.)

The Occult Explosion. New York: Freedland, Nat. Putnam's Sons, 1972.

The Black Arts. Cavendish, Richard. Capicorn Books, 1967. (Good reference book on various occult theologies, rituals, etc.)

The Satanic Rituals. La Vey, Anton.

The Satanic Bible. LaVey, Anton. N.Y.: Avon Books, 1969.

Satan Is Alive And Well On Planet Earth. Linsey, H. with Carlson, C.C., New York: Bantam Books, 1972.

Satan, Sorcery And Sex. Lawrence.

The Second Coming: Satanism In America. Lyons, Arthur.

Kingdom Of The Occult. Martin, Walter.

The Great Beast. Symonds, J. New York: Roy Publishers, 1952.

The Family. Sanders, Ed. New York: E.P. Dutton, 1971.

Into The Occult. Underwood, Peter.

The Sexual Psychopathology of Witchcraft. Masters, R., Julian Press, 1962.

The Occult. Wilson, Colin. 1971.

Hostage To The Devil. Martin, Malachi. 1976.

SELECTED READINGS ON OCCULT & RITUAL ABUSE (1980 to 1992)

By Silence Betrayed. Crewdson, John. 1988.

Hassan, S. **Combating Cult Mind Control.** Rochester, VT. Park Street Press, 1988.

Cults In America: Programmed For Paradise. Appel, Willa. New York, 1983. (Explores who joints cults and why. Outlines techniques of mind control).

Cults That Kill. Kahaner, Larry. 1988.

Ross, J.C. & Langone, M.D. **Cults: What Parents Should Know.** New York: Carol Publishing Group, 1988.

Dictionary of Mysticism and The Occult. Drury, Nevill. 1985.

High Risk. Magid, Dr. Ken & McKelvey, Carole. 1987.

People Of The Lie: The Hope For Healing Human Evil. Peck, M. Scott. Simon & Schuster, 1983.

Hudson, Pamela S. **Ritual Child Abuse: Discovery, Diagnosis And Treatment.** R. and E. Publishing, 1991.

The Ultimate Evil. Terry, Murry. 1987. (An investigation into America's most dangerous satanic cult).

Unspeakable Acts. Hollingsworth, Jan; Condon & Weed, 1986.

Presentation Outline Examples

The following presentation outline examples can be used as guides when facilitating a sexual abuse awareness lecture or discussion group:

SOME TYPES OF SEXUAL ABUSE

POTENTIAL BEHAVIORAL CLUES FOR
IDENTIFYING VICTIMS OF SEXUAL ABUSE

ABOUT A CHILD MOLESTER
(WHAT WE FEAR - WHAT IS KNOWN)

COPING STYLES OF YOUNG MALE VICTIMS

COMMON SURVIVOR EXPERIENCES

CREATING A CLIMATE THAT ALLOWS BOYS
TO DISCLOSE SEXUAL ABUSE

COMPONENTS OF HEALING FOR ADULT
INCEST AND SEXUAL ABUSE SURVIVORS

Some Types of Sexual Abuse

- The adult sexually touching the child (e.g., a hug that is more sexual than affectionate).
- Having the child touch the adult sexually.
- Photographing the child for sexual purposes.
- Sexualized talk.
- Showing the child pornographic materials or making them available to the child.
- Making fun of or ridiculing the child's sexual development, preferences or organs.
- The adult exposing his or her genitals to the child for sexual gratification.
- Masturbating or otherwise being sexual in front of the child.
- Voyeurism (e.g., watching a child dress or undress after puberty).
- Forcing overly rigid rules on dress or forcing the child to wear revealing clothes.
- Stripping a child to hit or spank, or getting sexual excitement out of hitting.
- Verbal or emotional abuse of a sexual nature.
- Having the child engage in sexual activity with animals.

Potential Behavioral Clues for
Identifying Victims of Abuse:

- Abrupt Mood Swings
- Depression
- Easily Distracted
- Irritability
- Emotionally Immature
- Isolated & Withdrawn
- Frustrated Easily
- Colitis
- Physically Violent
- Low Self-Esteem
- Multiple Personalities
- District of "Authority"
- Obesity
- Bulimia
- Forgetfulness
- Has Many Short-Term Relationships
- Overtly Controlling (in charge)
- Difficulty with Emotional Intimacy
- Pessimistic
- Acts Out Sexually
- Angry
- Suicidal
- Drug / Alcohol Addicted
- Inability to Trust
- No Sexual Interest At All
- Sexual Dysfunction
- Gaps in Childhood Memories
- Anorexia
- Ulcers
- Confused Sexual Preference / Identity
- Problems Being Touched or Held
- Out-of-Proportion Emotional Responses to Everyday Occurrences

Here are some additional traits that many victims / survivors share. They are:

- Guess at what normal behavior is
- Have difficulty following through on projects
- Lie when it would be just as easy to tell the truth
- Judge themselves without mercy
- Don't know how to play or have fun
- Take themselves too seriously
- Overreact to changes over which they have no control
- Need constant approval and affirmation
- Often feel different from other people
- Are either extremely responsible or irresponsible
- Are extremely loyal, even when the loyalty is undeserved

About A Child Molester

What We Fear	What Is Known
A Dangerous Stranger	Often a Relative or Friend of the Family
An Isolated Incident	Occurs Over & Over Again
Out of the Blue, Unexpected	A Situation that Develops Gradually Over a Period of Time
A Violent Attack	Subtle Rather Than Forced
A Kidnapping	Abuse Occurs in the Victim's Home or Other Familiar Setting
A Convicted Felon	Coach, Teacher, Priests / Nuns, Minister, Neighbor, Babysitter, Co-Worker, Scout Leaders, Etc.
Only Men	Female & Male Perpetrators
Homosexual Males	Majority are Heterosexual Males

About The Victim

What We Fear	What Is Known
Suffers Serious Emotional and Psychological Damage	Healing and Recovery are Possible with Counseling and Education
Unable to Maintain Intimate Relationship	Relationships, Friendship and Partnerships Possible
Victim will Become a Molester / Abuser	Many **DO NOT** Become Offenders but Advocates of Child Abuse Prevention
Males Become Homosexual if Abused by Older Male	No Substantial Research Data to Support this Assumption

Coping Styles Of Young Male Victims

Fight
- acting out, delinquency, tantrums
- promiscuity / highly sexualized behaviors (compulsive masturbation and sexual acting out)
- acting super-responsible
- using food as a protect (eating disorders)
- dreaming of revenge
- aggressions towards pets / animals
- mood swings / irritability
- overactivity
- fire-setting (arson)

Flight
- run away - marry young to leave home
- suicide or attempted suicide
- develop multiple personalities
- develop stress illnesses
- hypervigilant - sleep disturbances
- regressive behaviors - phobic behaviors

Numbing
- deny feelings - live in constant state of shock
- dissociation - use of alcohol / drugs
- school failure (due to attention and withdrawal)
- self-mutilation (detracts from internal pain)
- depression

Common Survivor Experiences

1. I didn't recall large portions of my childhood.

2. I experience drastic mood swings.

3. I am afraid to let out my anger, it could kill.

4. I have difficulty asking for help.

5. I am overwhelmed by changes in plans or schedules.

6. I am uncomfortable around persons "in authority".

7. I have acted out sexually in risky or unhealthy ways.

8. I have difficulty in remembering recent events / occasions.

9. I don't enjoy sex.

10. I don't trust many people.

11. I don't know how to relax.

12. I am often emotional and withdrawn.

Creating A Climate That Allows
Boys To Disclose Sexual Abuse

- Question children referred for aggressive behavior about the possibility of prior sexual abuse.
- Educate children about the possibility of males being victims.
- Question all siblings when abuse of one child is discovered.
- Offer male victims the same level of protection, treatment and concern as females.
- Have access to materials and resources designed for male victims.
- Educate those working in rape crisis and other hotlines about male sexual victimization. Recruit male survivors to assist.
- Counter the prevailing sex-role myths about the invincibility of the "real man" with more realistic roles for boys to emulate.
- Encourage older males to speak out about victimization experiences.

Components Of Healing For
Adult Incest / Sexual Abuse Survivors

1. Breaking the secrecy / undoing the isolation.
   A. Tell your story to a trustworthy person.
   B. Search for an appropriate qualified therapist.
   C. Join a support group for survivors.

2. Learning to set and achieve reasonable goals.

3. Learning positive coping skills (including ending addictions and compulsive behaviors).

4. Mobilize social support—establishing and reinforcing positive connections with people.

5. Breaking secrecy in the family.

6. Recognizing that recovery is an ongoing process.

7. Creating new meaning for past trauma—helping others.

Resource Catalogs

The following agencies offer catalogs which contain a variety of "Healing / Recovery" publications, pamphlets, audio / video tapes and related educational materials.

American Counseling Association
5999 Stevenson Ave.
Alexandria, VA 22304
(800) 347-6647

Channing L. Bete Co., Inc.
200 State Road
South Deerfield, MA 01373-0200
(800) 628-7733

Above and Beyond
P.O. Box 2672
Ann Arbor, MI 48106-2672

Ally Press Center
524 Orleans Street
St. Paul, MN 55107
(612) 291-2652, (800) 729-3002

Al-Anon Family Group Headquarters
P.O. Box 862, Midtown Station
New York, NY 10018-0862
(212) 302-7240

Forensic Mental Health Associates
7513 Pointview Circle
Orlando, FL 32836-6336
(508) 987-5119, (407) 351-2308

Full Circle Bookstore "Healing" Catalog
2205 Silver S.E.
Albuquerque, NM 87106
(505) 266-0022

Human Services Institute, Inc.
P.O. Box 20058
New York, NY 10025
(800) 366-7086

Haworth Press, Inc.
10 Alice Street
Binghamton, NY 13904-1580
(800) 342-9678
Clinical / Professional Publications

IBS Press, Inc.
744 Pier Ave.
Santa Monica, CA 90405
(800) 234-6485, (213) 450-6485

KidsRights
10100 Park Cedar Dr.
Charlotte, NC 28210
(704) 541-0100, (800) 892-KIDS

National Institute of Mental Health
Dept. of Health & Human Services
Room 15C-05, Public Health Service
Alcohol, Drug Abuse & Mental Health
Rockville, MD 20857

Lambda Rising News
1625 Connecticut Ave. NW
Washington, DC 20009
(202) 462-6969
Contemporary Gay / Lesbian literature

Lexington books - "Social issues" update
125 Spring St.
Lexington, MA 02173
(212) 819-7474, (800) 235-3565

Sidran Foundation Bookshelf
(Multiple Personality & Dissociation)
2328 W. Joppa Road, Suite #15
Lutherville, MD 21093

Monarch Resources
P.O. Box 1293
Torrance, CA 90505-0293
(310) 373-1958

National Committee for Prevention
of Child Abuse
332 S. Michigan Ave., #1600
Chicago, IL 60604
(312) 663-3520

Perrin & Treggett Booksellers
P.O. Box 190
Rutherford, NJ 07070
(800) 321-7912

Stern's Periodicals Press
5804 N. Magnolia St.
Chicago, IL 60660
(312) 561-2121, (312) 883-5100

Sage Periodicals Press
P.O. Box 5084
Newbury Park, CA 91359
(805) 499-0721

Safer Society Press
RR1, Box 24-B
Orwell, VT 05760-9756
(802) 897-7541

Step'n Stones
1327 C. Post Ave.
Torrance, CA 90501
(800) 266-7837

Springer Publishing Co.
536 Broadway
New York, NY 10012

UNIQUITY
P.O. Box 6
Galt, CA 95632
(209) 745-2111

Resource Organizations

Adults Molested As Children United
Giarretto Institute
P.O. Box 952
San Jose, CA 95108
(408) 453-7616

Anorexics & Bulimics Anonymous
4500 E. Pacific Coast Hwy, #330
Long Beach, CA 90804
(213) 597-4519

American Anorexia / Bulimia
   Association
133 Cedar Lane, Teaneck, NJ 07666
(201) 836-1800

American Professional Society on the
   Abuse of Children (APSAC)
332 S. Michigan Ave., #1600
Chicago, IL 60604
(312) 554-0166

Children of Alcoholics Foundation
200 Park Ave., 31st Floor
New York, NY 10166
(212) 949-1404

Cult Awareness Network
2421 W. Pratt Blvd.
Chicago, IL 60645
(312) 267-7777

C. Henry Kempe Center for
   Prevention & Treatment of Child
   Abuse and Neglect
1205 Oneida St. Denver, CO 80220
(303) 321-3963

International Cult Education Program
P.O. Box 1232 Gracie Station
New York, NY 10028
(212) 439-1550

MAZE, The (MPD)
P.O. Box 88722
Tukwila, WA 98138-2722

Multiple Personality Dignity
P.O. Box 4367
Boulder, CO 80306-4367

National Organization of
  Circumcision Information and
  Resource Centers
P.O. Box 2512
San Anselmo, CA 94979-2512
(415) 488-9883

National Organization for
  Victim Assistance
717 D Street, NW
Washington, DC 20004
(202) 232-6682

National Resource Center on
  Child Abuse
63 Inverness Dr.
East Englewood, CO 80112
(800) 227-5242 or (303) 792-9900

Nat. Resource Center on
  Child Sexual Abuse
107 Lincoln St.
Huntsville, AL 35801
(800) 543-7006 or (205) 534-6868
Professional inquiries only

National Self-Help Clearinghouse
City University of New York
33 W. 42nd St., #12222
New York, NY 10036
(212) 840-1259 For self-help group
listings

National Victim Center
307 W. 7th St., #1001
Fort Worth, TX 76102
(817) 877-3355

Office for Victims of Crime
633 Indian Ave., NW #1368
Washington, DC 20531
(212) 514-6444

Ritual Abuse Awareness Network
  Soceity
P.O. Box 29064 Delamont Station
1996 W. Broadway
Vancouver, BC
Canada V6J 5C2

Survivors of Childhood Abuse Program
P.O. Box 630
Hollywood, CA 90028

Victims of Clergy Abuse (VOCAL)
P.O. Box 1268
Wheeling, IL 60090

VOICES - Victims of Incest Can
  Emerge Survivors
P.O. Box 148309
Chicago, IL 60614
(312) 327-1500

Resource Newsletters

Family Violence & Sexual Assault
  Bulletin
1310 Clinic Dr. Tyler, TX 75701
(903) 595-6600

Gay/Lesbian Domestic
  Violence Newsletter
P.O. Box 14546
San Francisco, CA 94114

Healing Paths
P.O. Box 599
Coos Bay, OR 97420-0114

Incest Survivors Enlightened
  & Empowered
P.O. Box 82
Milton, VT 05468-3525

Incest Survivor Information Exchange
P.O. Box 3399
New Haven, CT 06515
(203) 235-4353

Incest Survivors Resource Network
P.O. Box 7375
Las Cruces, NM 88006-7375

Incest Resources, Inc.
Cambridge Women's Center
46 Pleasant St. Cambridge, MA 02139
(617) 354-8807

Many Voices
P.O. Box 2639
Cincinnati, OH 45201-2639
(Self-help publication for persons
w/MPD)

M.U.L.T.I.P.L.E.
P.O. Box 10224
Marina Del Rey, CA 90292

MPD Reaching Out c/o
Public Relations Department
Royal Ottawa Hospital
1145 Carling Ave.
Ottawa, Ontario Canada K1Z 7K4

Multiple Personality Dignity
P.O. Box 4367
Boulder, CO 80306-4367

Survivors of Clergy Abuse
P.O. Box 40676
Albuquerque, NM 87196

Survivors of Female Incest Emerge
  (SOFIE)
P.O. Box 2794
Renton, WA 98056-2794

The Survivors Network
P.O. Box 80058
Albuquerque, NM 87198

Virginia Child Protection Newsletter
  (VCPN)
c/o James Madison University
Department of Psychology
Harrisonburg, VA 22807

Write to Heal c/o WordsRight
P.O. Box 358
Fair Oaks, CA 95628-0358

Hotlines

National Child Abuse Hotline
(800) 422-4453

National Center for Missing & Exploited Children
(800) 843-5678

National Cocaine-Abuse Hotline
(800) 262-2463

National Council on Child Abuse & Family Violence
(800) 222-2000

National Institute of Drug Abuse Hotline
(800) 662-4357

Runaway Hotline
(800) 621-4000